THE
SURRENDERED
WIFE

A PRACTICAL GUIDE FOR FINDING
INTIMACY, PASSION, AND PEACE WITH A MAN

LAURA DOYLE

A Fireside Book
Published by Simon & Schuster
New York   London   Toronto   Sydney   Singapore

FIRESIDE
Rockefeller Center
1230 Avenue of the Americas
New York, NY 10020

FIRESIDE and colophon are registered trademarks
of Simon & Schuster, Inc.

Designed by William P. Rusto

Manufactured in the United States of America

10   9   8   7   6   5   4

Library of Congress Cataloging-in-Publication Data

Doyle, Laura.
    The surrendered wife : a practical guide for finding intimacy,
passion, and peace with a man / Laura Doyle.
        p.   cm.
    "A Fireside book."
    1. Marriage.   2. Wives—Conduct of life.   3. Control
(Psychology)   4. Submissiveness.   I. Title.
HQ734.D79 2001
306.81—dc21   00-045010

ISBN 0-7432-0444-1

ACKNOWLEDGMENTS

Special thanks to all the women in the original Surrendered Circle, especially Lynnae Bennett and Christine Gordon, who were the first ones brave enough to take this plunge. Christine also has my eternal thanks for her expert editing. What would I do without her? Glad I don't have to think about *that!*

Speaking of expert editors, I'm incredibly lucky that this book fell into the hands of Doris Cooper at Simon & Schuster, who was visionary enough to see its potential. She is wonderfully encouraging and motivating—and amazingly thorough.

Of course, I never would have met Doris if I didn't have the best agent in the world: Jimmy Vines. Thanks, Jimmy!

I'm also thankful to my sisters Hannah and Katie, who let me draft them into surrendering and provided thoughtful insights. My brother, John, was a wonderful source of support and inspiration while I was writing this book.

Most of all, I'm grateful to my beloved husband, John Doyle. He helped me to become my best self, and made me laugh all along the way. I still say I'm a little luckier.

For John

THE
SURRENDERED
WIFE

CONTENTS

INTRODUCTION

> *"To fall in love is easy, even to remain in it is not difficult;
> our human loneliness is cause enough. But it is a hard quest
> worth making to find a comrade through whose steady
> presence one becomes steadily the person one desires to be."*
> —ANNA LOUISE STRONG

WHY WOULD A WOMAN SURRENDER?

When I was newly married at twenty-two, I had no idea I would ever call myself a surrendered wife. At that time, the very phrase would have repulsed me.

I did know that marriage was risky because I had watched my parents go through a brutal divorce. Still, I was hopeful that I could do better. I was amazed that my husband, John, could love me as much as he did, and part of me believed we could make our marriage work simply because it was born of so much goodness.

At first our marriage was blissful. Then, I started to see John's imperfections more glaringly, and I began correcting him. It was my way of helping him to improve. From my point of view, if he

13

would just be more ambitious at work, more romantic at home, and clean up after himself, everything would be fine. I told him as much.

He didn't respond well. And, it's no wonder. What I was really trying to do was *control* John. The harder I pushed, the more he resisted, and we both grew irritable and frustrated. While my intentions were good, I was clearly on the road to marital hell. In no time I was exhausted from trying to run my life and his. Even worse, I was becoming estranged from the man who had once made me so happy. Our marriage was in serious trouble and it had only been four years since we'd taken our vows.

My loneliness was so acute I was willing to try anything to cure it. I went to therapy, where I learned that I often used control as a defense. I read John Gray's *Men Are from Mars, Women Are from Venus,* which gave me some understanding of the different ways men and women communicate and approach life. I talked to other women to find out what worked in their marriages.

One friend told me she let her husband handle all of the finances, and what a relief that was for her. Another one told me she tried never to criticize her husband, no matter how much he seemed to deserve it. I decided I would try to follow in these women's footsteps as an "experiment" in my marriage. I desperately wanted to save the relationship, and I also hoped to rescue my self-respect, which was fading with each episode of anger and frustration I unleashed on John.

Little did I know that I was taking the first baby steps in surrendering and that doing so would renew our marital tranquility and my self-respect. Today I call myself a surrendered wife because when I stopped trying to control the way John did everything and started trusting him implicitly, I began to have the marriage I've always dreamed of. The same thing will happen to you if you follow the principles in this book.

None of us feels good about ourselves when we're nagging,

critical, or controlling. I certainly didn't. The tone of my voice alone would make me cringe with self-recrimination. Through surrendering, you will find the courage to gradually stop indulging in these unpleasant behaviors and replace them with dignified ones.

You will also have more time and energy to focus on what's most important to you. Whether your desire is to have a more harmonious family, run a top corporation, or both, you'll feel increasing pride as you realize your goals faster than ever before. Surrendering has a way of bringing out the best in us, both as individuals and as wives, which is why it's so worth doing.

HOW INTIMATE IS YOUR MARRIAGE?			
DO YOU:	RARELY	SOMETIMES	FREQUENTLY
1. Feel superior to your husband?			
2. Nag your husband?			
3. Commiserate with other wives about your husband?			
4. Hear yourself say, "I told my husband . . ."			
5. Think that everything would be fine if your husband would do what you tell him to do?			
6. Eavesdrop on your husband's conversations?			
7. Feel like the only adult in the family?			
8. Feel overburdened in parenting your children?			
9. Do things for your husband that he is capable of doing for himself?			
10. Have recurring anxiety and depression?			
11. Feel exhausted?			
12. Find either of you are disinterested in sex?			

DO YOU:	RARELY	SOMETIMES	FREQUENTLY
13. Feel resentful or jealous about your husband's victories in life?			
14. Reject or criticize his gifts?			
15. Fantasize about divorce or life with a man who would better match you?			
16. Discount the reasons you chose your husband in the first place?			
17. Feel hopeless about your marriage because your needs have gone unmet for so long?			
18. Have a hard time trusting your husband in even small matters?			
19. Find yourself trying to control your husband?			
20. Get angry with your husband when he makes a poor decision?			

Quiz Scoring: How Intimate is Your Marriage?

To total your score, give yourself:
- *5 points for each "rarely"*
- *3 points for each "sometimes"*
- *1 point for each "frequently"*
- *Add all three columns together for a final score (somewhere between 20 and 100)*

If your score is 35 or less:
  What intimacy?

You're probably wondering what the heck you ever saw in this guy! But not to worry—the tenderness you seek may just be dormant. If you can remember the reasons you agreed to marry him in the first place and start respecting him for those reasons, you can still have the marriage you always dreamed was possible. Find the courage to stop controlling your husband today. You won't be sorry. You can transform your marriage, starting now.

16

IF YOUR SCORE IS 36 TO 60:

Overworked and Underappreciated

It's hard to tell because you make it look easy, but you're doing too much and you need a break. Start to take better care of yourself and ask for help more often. Your vulnerability will be rewarded if your husband feels respected. Thank your husband for his contributions and you will be well on your way to igniting passion and achieving intimacy.

IF YOUR SCORE IS 61 OR ABOVE:

Congratulations!

Your marriage is very intimate and passionate. You found a man you respect, and the two of you have a positive impact on each other. This union is a healthy mix of individuality and togetherness. You practice good self-care, you're quick to apologize, and he adores you for it.

THE RETURN OF THE MAN WHO WOOED ME

"Our thoughts, our words, and deeds are the threads of the net which we throw around ourselves."

— SWAMI VIVEKANANDA

*T*here was no single moment when the surrendered lightbulb went off in my head. Instead, I changed little by little. I experimented, first by keeping my mouth shut—and sometimes even my eyes—when John drove. When we arrived in one piece, I decided that I would always trust him behind the wheel, no matter how strong my urge to control.

Next, I stopped buying his clothes (yes, even his underwear), even though I worried that he wouldn't buy any for himself. (I was wrong.) I learned what *not* to do from making painful mistakes, like criticizing the way he maintained the cars, which made me feel like my mother when she was cranky and caused John to watch TV for four straight hours, avoiding me. I prayed for wisdom, and took more baby steps towards approaching the relationship without control.

Slowly but surely, things started to change.

As I stopped bossing him around, giving him advice, burying him in lists of chores to do, criticizing his ideas and taking over every situation as if he couldn't handle it, something magical happened. The union I dreamed of appeared.

The man who wooed me was back.

We were intimate again. Instead of keeping a running list of complaints about how childish and irresponsible he was, I felt genuine gratitude and affection for John. We were sharing our responsibilities without blame or resentment. Instead of bickering all the time, we were laughing together, holding hands, dancing in the kitchen, and enjoying an electrifying closeness that we hadn't had for years.

For our ninth wedding anniversary, I changed my last name to match my husband's. "Now that I know him a little better, I figure I'll give it a shot," I joked to my friends. What I really meant was that I wanted to be intimate with John in a way that I never was before. I wanted to do something that symbolized my tremendous respect for him, and to acknowledge outwardly an inward shift. This was the natural development of a path I had started some time ago without realizing it.

At first, I felt uneasy when I held my tongue instead of expressing my opinion about everything. Restraining myself from correcting my husband felt like trying to write with my left hand. Life had become awkward!

But there were positive results. Over time, I formed new habits. When I slipped back into my old ways, I stopped to ask myself, "Which do I want more: to have control of every situation or to have an intimate marriage?"

Naturally, emotional connection, lack of tension, dignity, having kindness, and being able to relax always trumped getting the chores done or having things my way all the time. To remind myself of my new priorities, I adopted the word "surrender" as my mantra, because it was shorter and more to the point than saying, "stop trying to control everything." I repeated "surrender" to myself silently over and over again.

BECOMING YOUR BEST SELF

> *"Virtue herself is her own fairest reward."*
> —SILIUS ITALICUS

*S*urrendering to your husband is not about returning to the fifties or rebelling against feminism.

This book isn't about dumbing down or being rigid.

It's certainly not about subservience.

It's about following some basic principles that will help you change your habits and attitudes to restore intimacy to your marriage. It's about having a relationship that brings out the best in both of you, and growing together as spiritual beings. Surrendering is both gratifying and terrifying, but the results—peace, joy, and feeling good about yourself and your marriage—are proven.

The basic principles of a surrendered wife are that she:

- Relinquishes inappropriate control of her husband
- Respects her husband's thinking
- Receives his gifts graciously and expresses gratitude for him

- Expresses what she wants without trying to control him
- Relies on him to handle household finances
- Focuses on her own self-care and fulfillment

A surrendered wife is:

- Vulnerable where she used to be a nag
- Trusting where she used to be controlling
- Respectful where she used to be demeaning
- Grateful where she used to be dissatisfied
- Has faith where she once had doubt

A surrendered wife has abundance where she was once impoverished, and typically has more disposable income and more satisfying, connected sex than she did before she surrendered.

My sister, Hannah Childs, related the philosophy of the surrendered wife to her experience as a ballroom dance teacher. "In marriage," she said, "as in ballroom dancing, one must lead and the other must follow. This is not to say that both roles are not equally important. It is rare that I find a woman who can resist 'backleading.'"

"I did everything he did," Ginger Rogers once said about Fred Astaire. "And I did it backwards, and in high heels." Although Fred and Ginger were equally skilled and talented dancers, if they had both tried to lead (or follow), they would have been pulling each other in opposite directions. Quite simply, they would not be in sync, but rather would be tripping over each other and eventually pulling apart. Instead, Ginger let Fred lead her, trusting that he was making her look good and keeping her from harm. Instead of Fred diminishing her, Ginger allowed him to be the foil for her talent.

I want my husband to bring out my very best, too.

The Origin of Control

> *"One's mind, once stretched by a new idea, never regains its original dimensions."*
> —Oliver Wendell Holmes

*L*ong before we fell in love and got married, every controlling wife suffered disappointments. At a young age, some of our most basic needs went unmet. This could be the result of any number of things: the untimely death of a parent or the frustrations of a family member's addiction. It could have been the consequence of relatively small things, like not getting the tennis shoes we desperately needed to fit in at school, or having to adjust to less attention because of the arrival of another sibling. Whatever the cause, we then made an erroneous conclusion that no one would ever take care of us the way we wanted.

We embraced a childish belief that if we were always in charge, things were more likely to go our way.

Some of us were so used to living in fear about not getting what we needed that we never even noticed our quickened pulse and shallow breathing. We normalized this level of terror and our accompanying auto-response: Taking control. We believed that the more we could control people around us—husbands, siblings and friends alike—the better off we would be.

Just as fish are always the last to discover they are in the ocean, those of us who survive by trying to control things around us are often the last to recognize our behavior. We tell ourselves that we are trying to instruct, improve, help others, or do things efficiently—never that we are so afraid of the unpredictable that we do everything in our power to ensure a certain outcome.

For instance, I thought I was merely making helpful suggestions when I told my husband that he should ask for a raise. When I urgently exclaimed that we should have turned right instead of left while riding in a friend's car who knew perfectly well how to get to our destination, I reasoned that I was trying to save time and avoid traffic. When I tried to convince my brother that he really should get some therapy, I justified butting into his life as wanting "to be there for him."

All of these justifications were merely elaborate covers for my inability to trust others. If I had trusted that my husband was earning as much money as he could, I wouldn't have emasculated him by implying that I found him lacking ambition. If I had trusted my friend to get us to our destination in a reasonable time, I wouldn't have barked out orders about where to turn, leaving a cold frost on the inside of the car. If I had trusted my brother to make his own way in the world, he would've felt more inclined to continue to share the emotional milestones of his life with me.

Trusting is magical because people tend to live up to our expectations. If you make it clear to your husband that you expect him to screw up at work, wreck the car, or neglect his health, you are setting a negative expectation. If on the other hand, you expect him to succeed, he is much more likely to do just that.

To trust someone means you put your full confidence in them, the way Robert Redford's character in the movie *The Horse Whisperer* trusted a teenager behind the wheel of his truck for the first time—by resting in the passenger seat with his hat over his eyes. Trusting someone means you anticipate the best outcome—not the worst—when he's in charge. When you trust, you don't need to double-check, make back-up plans or be vigilant because you're not expecting any danger. You can sleep with both eyes shut, knowing that everything's going to be fine.

It bears repeating: When you trust, you are anticipating the best outcome.

Those of us who have trouble trusting others when every rational indicator says that we are safe are reacting to our own fear. We may be afraid that we won't get what we need, or that we'll get it too late. We may fear that we'll spend too much money, or have to do extra work. It could be, and often is, that we fear loneliness, boredom, or discomfort. If you are like me and find yourself driven to correct, criticize, and conquer a partner, then you are reacting to *your* fears. Whatever the situation, if you do not react to your fear of the outcome, you don't need to try to dominate, manipulate, or control it.

As it turns out, my fears were a conditioned response I had developed over the years to hide my own vulnerability—the soft underbelly that exposes me to both the greatest pain and the greatest pleasure. I hid my softness as much as I could because I believed it was unattractive. Ironically, the people I found most endearing and easiest to connect with had the ability to expose their real fears, joys, guilt, needs, and sadness. I was drawn to their openness and warmth. I found them engaging.

When I was choosing to control over allowing myself to be vulnerable, I was doing so at the expense of intimacy. What I know now is that control and intimacy are opposites. If I want one, I can't have the other. Without being vulnerable, I can't have intimacy. Without intimacy, there can be no romance or emotional connection. When I am vulnerable with my husband, the intimacy, passion, and devotion seem to flow naturally.

Today I try to relinquish control as much as I can and allow myself to be vulnerable. Unfortunately, I still don't do this perfectly, but it doesn't seem to matter. Just making intimacy my priority—rather than control—by practicing the principles described in this book, has transformed my marriage into a passionate, romantic union.

MY BAGS WERE ALWAYS PACKED

❋

> *"If you can't say something nice, don't say anything at all."*
> — MOM

A friend of mine described herself in her marriage as mentally "having her bags packed and her running shoes on" at all times so she could get her things together and flee in just a matter of minutes. She was always ready to pursue a life in which she could provide everything that she needed for herself without *his* help.

My therapist reminded me that when I first started coming to see her, I was the same way. I often felt I would be better off divorced or with another man who was more fastidious or considerate. With the husband of my imagination, I wouldn't have to plan, arrange, organize, and check up on everything. My rotten attitude cast gloom over the relationship. I was always on edge, so that the slightest problem seemed like reason enough to end this marriage and hope for a better one next time. At the time, I felt so pained and self-righteous that honoring my wedding vows seemed unimportant. Today my friends laugh at me when I tell them this because it seems so ridiculous that I was ready to toss out my perfectly wonderful husband.

WHY THIS BOOK ISN'T CALLED
THE SURRENDERED HUSBAND

"Some people find fault as if it were buried treasure."
— FRANCIS O'WALSH

If you're a wife who feels overwhelmed, lonely and responsible for everything, this book is perfect for you. If you can admit that you frequently or sometimes control, nag, or criticize your husband, then it is up to you and you alone to take the actions described here to restore intimacy to your marriage and dignity and peace to yourself.

I am *not* saying that you are responsible for every problem in your marriage. You are not. Your husband has plenty of areas he could improve too, but that's nothing you can control. You can't make him change—you can only change yourself. The good news is that since you've identified the behaviors that contribute to your problems, you can begin to solve them. Rather than wasting time thinking about what my husband should do, I prefer to keep all my energy for improving *my* happiness. The point of my journey was to give up controlling behavior, and to look inward instead of outward.

I encourage you to do the same.

HOW OTHER WOMEN SURRENDERED

*hortly after I started practicing the steps of The Surrendered Wife, I had the opportunity to share this philosophy with some friends who brought the principles to their marriages. Not only did they validate the process, they added further wonder to it. They, too, experienced inspiring transformations. Soon a group of five of us—a Surrendered Circle—was meeting in my living room once a month. The circle grew quickly as women I had never met began calling me to learn more about how they could revitalize their marriages. When our size threatened to exceed the capacity of my living room, I closed the meetings to newcomers and started Surrendered Wife Workshops, which teach women the skills and help them form the habits they need to surrender successfully. (You can learn more about workshops in your area by calling 1-800-466-2028 or visiting www.surrenderedwife.com). Still more women came forward wanting to know how to surrender to their husbands. Now Surrendered Circles, which offer free support, meet in local communities and on the Internet.

Today there are thousands of women practicing the principles of The Surrendered Wife. They, too, have rekindled the love and closeness that had been dormant for years in their marriages, and gotten a break from feeling responsible for everything. In the pages of this book, you will see glimpses of stories from the women I've met through the circle, my workshop and The Surrendered Wife web site. All the anecdotes are true, although the names and some other details have been changed to protect their privacy.

WHEN NOT TO SURRENDER AND GET OUT

*Y*our husband does things that get on your very last nerve. I know this because I have a husband myself, and, like yours, he is a mere mortal with numerous imperfections. At times I found his shortcomings so big that I thought I couldn't live with him for another day.

As it turns out, my husband is one of the good guys.

But how do you know if your husband is a good guy? When should you get out?

There are some situations in which a wife should not trust her husband. Under these particular circumstances, I suggest separation or divorce—not surrender. Only you can judge whether you are in one of these situations.

Before you surrender check to see if any of the following apply to your situation:

1. Do not surrender to a man who is physically abusive to you.
When your safety is threatened, there can be no intimacy. I urge you to leave your relationship as quickly as possible if your husband has done any of the following:

- Hit you
- Kicked you
- Punched you
- Physically forced you to be sexual against your will

Get help from friends, therapists or clergy and get out. Start making plans and taking action *today*. For further assistance, call the National Domestic Violence/Abuse Hotline at 1-800-799-7233.

2. *Do not surrender to a man who is physically abusive to your children.*

If your husband is inappropriately violent or sexual with your kids, you must protect them immediately. The sooner you leave this relationship, the better your chances of getting into a relationship with a healthy, loving man who will *protect,* rather than *harm,* you and your children. (Spanking a child as discipline, however controversial or unacceptable to you, does not qualify as physical abuse. Just because the two of you disagree about corporal punishment does not give you justification to leave the relationship.)

3. *Do not surrender to a man who has an active addiction.*

A man with an addiction to a substance such as alcohol or drugs, or to an activity such as gambling, cannot be trusted. I can offer little hope of intimacy in this situation, as he will always serve his addiction ahead of your safety and happiness.

Of course, it's not always easy to identify an addiction. If you are uncertain, but suspect that he has an active addiction, find some quiet time and space to contemplate this question. Has his substance abuse or gambling ever interfered with your relationship? Would he keep drinking, using, or betting even if he knew it was making you uncomfortable and lonely? Has he tried to stop in the past, only to take it up again?

Ask your gut, and listen carefully to the response. If you answer yes to one or more of these questions, your husband probably has an active addiction. If this is the case, remind yourself that you deserve to be the first priority to your husband. Remember that the sooner you reject what is inappropriate for you, the sooner you will be able to form a relationship with someone who will treat you like a princess.

If you are having trouble deciding whether your husband falls into the category of a practicing addict, consider contacting Al-Anon, a free program designed to help the family members of alcoholics and addicts. Al-Anon has meetings all over the world, and is listed in your local phone book.

4. Do not surrender to a man who is chronically unfaithful.

A man who has been unfaithful time and again, despite promises to the contrary, cannot be trusted. You deserve to be with a man who is sexual and romantic with you and you alone. So, if your husband is not capable of doing that, your best chance of true intimacy is to end the marriage and look for a man who *can* be faithful.

Having said that, a past extramarital affair does not automatically make your husband a chronic philanderer. It may have been his inappropriate reaction to years of emasculation and criticism from his wife. That doesn't make the affair your fault; it's still his responsibility to communicate with you and to keep his vows. However, your marriage can heal from this type of infidelity once you begin surrendering, if your husband is willing to recommit himself to monogamy.

WHAT ABOUT VERBAL ABUSE?

*W*omen sometimes ask me if they should leave a husband who is verbally abusive. This is an important question because verbal abuse crushes your sense of self-worth over time, just as physical abuse does. You certainly don't deserve to be belittled. Fortunately, as you will see, respecting your husband and refraining from controlling him will put an end to his hurtful words—as long as he doesn't fall into one of the four categories above.

Here's why.

If he is insulting, check to see if you have a *culture* of verbal abuse in your relationship. This kind of mistreatment is very rarely a one-way street, and is often a man's way of protecting himself against ongoing insults and emasculation. Again, it is *not* your fault if your husband is verbally abusive, but your behavior certainly influences him.

One woman complained to me that her husband had called her terrible names while they argued and that his verbal abuse was simply intolerable. As we talked some more, she told me some of the dreadful things *she* had said to *him* during this same argument. At first, she objected to the idea of apologizing for her disrespect because *he* had not yet apologized.

Rather than try to convince her that they both needed to apologize, I decided to take a different tack. I asked her what was more important: his apology (and her ego) or restored harmony. It didn't take long for her to admit that it was the latter. It wasn't long before she was willing to break the ice.

Her husband responded by apologizing for what he had said in anger, and harmony was indeed restored.

Over time, intimacy, respect and gratitude completely replaced verbal attacks in that relationship, as well as many others, as the wife continued to surrender. The same can happen in your marriage.

DECIDE IF YOUR MAN DESERVES YOUR TRUST

> *"We all suffer from the preoccupation that there exists . . . in the loved one, perfection."*
> — SIDNEY POITIER

*I*f your husband *doesn't* fall into one of the categories above, then you are married to one of the good guys. Not a perfect husband, but one who is capable of loving you and cherishing you— one who has the potential to help you feel great about yourself and your marriage.

Really.

If you are like most women, you are already thinking about how your life will fall apart if you stop controlling your husband. Perhaps you feel you cannot refrain from teaching or correcting your husband because then the children will lack discipline, or because you will go broke, or because you firmly believe the marriage will never change. If you are thinking there is some reason you can't follow this suggestion, you are not alone.

That's what we all think.

I know what I'm suggesting is difficult. I know it doesn't seem fair. It didn't seem fair to me that I had to work so hard to change while my husband continued to sit around watching television, but your husband will have to make big changes too. In fact, he will have to transform in order to stay in step with you as you leave the bumpy road of *not* trusting him and steer onto the smoother road of having faith in him. He will have to rise to new levels to meet this remarkable occasion.

He will have to listen to his own inner voice of conviction instead of relying on yours to tell him when he's not doing something right. He will need to use his own mind to figure out what's best for his family rather than reluctantly carrying out your subtle or not-so-subtle orders. He will be taking on far more responsibility than he ever has before. He will change as soon as you begin practicing the principles of The Surrendered Wife.

1

RESPECT THE MAN YOU MARRIED
BY LISTENING TO HIM

> *"Respect a man, he will do the more."*
> —JAMES HOWELL, 1659

Respect the man you married by listening to him without criticizing him, insulting him, laughing at him or making fun of him. Even if you disagree with him, do not dismiss his ideas.

If you have said or done something disrespectful, apologize for that specific incident. Acknowledge his response without further comment and be aware of your impulse to criticize or make a negative comment.

*I*n marriage, as in nature, water seeks its own level: we marry men who match us.

That means that respecting your husband is also a form of self-respect: It's a way of acknowledging that you made a wise and thoughtful choice to marry a man who deserves your love and esteem. If you treat him disrespectfully, you're saying that you made a poor choice and that you settled for someone beneath you.

For years I secretly believed I had married below myself, but I was wrong. In reality, this delusion was a convenient way for me to blame John for everything that went wrong. Perhaps you do the same thing.

Karen's husband ran a large corporation and earned a six-figure income. A few days before his birthday, he put a note on the counter with the one thing he most wanted his wife to give him: Respect. The same request is made in a variety of forms in households the world over, because men desperately crave respect from their wives. That makes it one of the greatest gifts we can give our husbands.

If you don't think your husband deserves *your* respect, ask yourself what it was you saw in him that made you marry him in the first place. At that time you trusted and admired him. Chances are he's not all that different now than he was then, and therefore is still worthy of your admiration.

HONOR HIS CHOICE OF SOCKS AND STOCKS

> *"Men are born to succeed, not to fail."*
> — HENRY DAVID THOREAU

So what does it mean to respect your partner? It means that you accept his choices, big and small, even if you don't agree with them. You honor his choice of socks and stocks, food and friendships, art and attitudes. You listen to him and have regard for his ideas, suggestions, family and work. That doesn't mean you have to make the same choices—just that you accept his.

When you respect your husband, you treat him like an intelligent adult rather than an irresponsible child. You use a tone becoming of a calm woman, not a frantic shrew.

Respecting your husband means that you don't tear him down. For example, telling him how to load the dishwasher is insulting. You might as well be saying, "You mean you can't even do something as easy as that?" Naturally, comments like that stifle intimacy.

Respect means that when he takes the wrong freeway exit you don't correct him by telling him where to turn. It means that if he keeps going in the wrong direction you will go past the state line and still not correct what he's doing. In fact, no matter what your husband does, you will not try to teach, improve, or correct him.

That is the essence of a surrendered wife.

Respect Breeds Intimacy

So what does respect have to do with intimacy?

When your husband feels secure in your opinion of him, he doesn't have to second-guess or steel himself because he's expecting you to pounce on him. When he knows you are on his side, he can relax and feel confident in himself.

Most importantly, when he knows you won't shoot an arrow in his Achilles' heel, he can let down his guard. Having that sense of safety will make it possible for him to share his innermost thoughts with you, and *that's* where you'll find intimacy. He may speak about the values he hopes to impart to the children, what he's imagining the two of you will do when you're old, or tell you about how he lost a dog he loved as a kid. He might talk about what he imagines it would be like to live on a ranch, go to the moon or add a second story to the house. Intimacy is made up of lots of little tender conversations—sometimes silly, sometimes solemn—that he wouldn't have with anyone else in the world. In fact, the actual details of the conversation are less important than the fact that the conversation is happening and connecting you spiritually.

But how exactly do you find your way to those tender conversations if you haven't had them in a while? How do you muster the gumption to become respectful when you're in the habit of nipping at him? Just as I did—by taking small steps until your habits have changed. You've already begun to raise your consciousness by reading this book, which is a great start. Later on in this chapter, I'll describe what disrespect looks like and feels like so you can start to see it in yourself. Just being able to identify disrespect helped me stay focused on the goal of respecting my husband,

which went a long way toward helping me find the intimate relationship I always wanted.

PRESERVING YOUR DIGNITY

*D*isrespecting your husband's choices on a regular basis is
like pricking him repeatedly with little pins. Imagine living with a
porcupine and you've got the idea of what it's like for him.

It's no fun to be the porcupine either. You find that your lover
doesn't want to get close to you because you're so prickly. Shed-
ding those prickers by treating your life partner with respect is a
gift for him, but it also dramatically improves your self-respect because your husband will reach out to you, making you feel loved
and wanted. Instead of having the unpleasant feeling of always
nagging or arguing, you hear yourself sounding more virtuous and
mature. You won't be haunted by the horror of wondering if
you've become your mother on her worst day. Since you didn't
much respect her when she ordered everyone around, you don't
much respect yourself when you hear it coming out of your own
mouth either.

I remember how unattractive and shameful I felt when I would
boss John and complain. In the middle of my tirade, I thought I
was saying what had to be said, but my self-respect deteriorated
with each harsh word. No matter how justified I felt in yelling or
correcting, I inevitably beat myself up afterwards, and of course
that only made me feel worse.

Now, I treat my husband respectfully not only to cultivate
closeness in our marriage, but also to preserve my dignity. I don't
miss the hostility hangovers.

THE "I WAS JUST TRYING TO HELP" SYNDROME

A lot of us have an unconscious refrain jingling in our heads that goes like this: "I know better than he does . . . I will help him do it right." With this background music, we quickly develop an air of superiority. We feel qualified to instruct our husbands on how to vacuum the carpet, talk to the children, and negotiate with his colleagues. All the while we tell ourselves that we are simply *helping.*

Unfortunately, "helping" in wife language translates into "controlling" in husband language. All those comments about how everything should be done are actually daggers of disrespect. Our generous "help" goes completely unappreciated, which makes us resentful. Somehow, we get so used to correcting our husbands that we don't even hear the harshness in our own comments, or notice how much we sound like a nag rather than the affectionate lover we set out to be.

THE MOTHER COMPLEX

> *You see an awful lot of smart guys with dumb women, but*
> *you hardly ever see a smart woman with a dumb guy.*
> — ERICA JONG

*I*f you feel as if you are the only adult in the family, think about this: Your husband manages to communicate, problem-solve, and produce in his job. Clearly he has the skills to do the same at home. So why doesn't he? Whenever we feel as if we have an extra child instead of a husband, it's because we're treating our husbands like little boys instead of capable men.

When I correct, criticize, or tell my husband what to do I automatically become his mother in that moment, which means he doesn't see me as his lover. There's no greater turn-off for me than seeing him as a helpless little boy and there's no bigger intimacy killer for him than feeling like he's with his mother. Your husband may not say so, but he feels the same way.

Your husband won't tell you he feels emasculated when you correct his behavior. He won't say that when you use that tone it gives him the same aggravated feeling he used to get when he was a teenager fantasizing about going someplace where no one would bother him. He certainly won't tell you when he finds you as sexually unappealing as he finds his mother.

Instead, the cold war begins.

When you let him know you don't think he'll make good decisions, he reverts to his boyhood ways and makes a mental note to give up to some degree, because he can never meet your standards. He may even agree with you subconsciously, and retreat from the activity entirely.

Who can blame him?

When men feel disrespected, they withdraw. Before I surrendered, my husband watched a lot of TV. Yours may find playing golf, working longer hours or fixing up old cars in the garage more appealing than being with you. Sure, there's some satisfaction in letting your husband know what you really think, but the price of that satisfaction is high: You have just isolated yourself from him and created your own bubble of loneliness.

Treating your husband with respect makes him want to be around you more, talk to you more, share more deeply, and make love to you more passionately. It can't hurt to remind him (and yourself) that you recognize you've married a clever, capable man.

THE CURE FOR THE COMMON COLD WAR

f you're like me, you've often wished you could be more respectful of your husband—if only he seemed up to the responsibility. The problem is you'll never know if he is until you give him the chance.

Perhaps you forget to trust and respect your partner because you are so accustomed to calling the shots at work that it's second nature to keep doing it when you get home. Maybe it shook your faith when he rear-ended a car on the freeway, and you have felt the need to caution him about driving ever since. You might have been disappointed to learn that he keeps a balance on the credit cards and pays interest that you feel is unnecessary. Whatever your reasons for not accepting the way your husband does things—and some of them are probably valid—you will still pay the high price of lost intimacy for insulting him. What's more important to you: having your watchful eye on everything or enjoying the warmth of intimacy? Recognize that those are your choices.

Once you've made the choice to respect him, you've made a powerful turn on the road to transforming your marriage and given yourself new rules for the road ahead. This is comparable to learning to drive a car. You make the decision to follow the rules of the road by stopping at a red light or putting your signal on to turn, because that is what you must do to get along with the other traffic on the road. If you stop at red lights only when you feel like it, ultimately you will crash. The same is true for getting along in your marriage: You're going to have to yield even when you don't feel like it to avoid a conflict.

One way to bite your tongue when you feel he's being immature or stubborn is to remind yourself that you are taking the high road. Sure, it would be easy to jab him, but instead find the grace to be generous. You can do it. Recall an occasion when your husband was thoughtful, courageous or self-sacrificing. Keep that picture in your mind so you resist the temptation to criticize him.

Since I don't have control over his path—only mine—if I don't take the high road we are both at our worst, and intimacy is nowhere to be found. If I take the high road, I am at my best. My chances for intimacy are at their greatest.

"EATING WORDS HAS NEVER GIVEN ME INDIGESTION."

That's what Winston Churchill said, and I can vouch for it.

Just as you may run a red light occasionally, you will also treat your husband less-than-respectfully at times, because no one is perfect. It is important, however, to apologize when you realize you haven't been so courteous. Therefore, a critical aspect of respecting your husband is catching yourself when you slip and letting him know that you regret it.

In the beginning, you'll probably find yourself having to apologize a lot: every time you roll your eyes at his idea, make an unsolicited suggestion about what he's wearing, or tell him what to say on the phone. Apologizing may be frustrating, but it's essential because it signals to your husband that you respect him. Even if you don't feel sorry, do your best to apologize when you're critical, bossy, nagging, or dismissing. This will feel odd—perhaps even dishonest—at first. Still, I suggest that you take this leap and act as if you do respect your husband. This is a powerful practice, because it takes your focus away from what you don't hold in high regard to the things that you do admire. The next thing you know, you will start to feel genuine respect for him.

When you apologize, be sure to reference the specific situation. For instance, you might say, "I apologize for being disrespectful when I criticized the way you were helping Taylor with her homework." Next, allow him to respond. The temptation to comment on the original situation in response to what he says will be enormous.

Don't do it.

You might be tempted to follow up the apology by saying, "It's just that you need to be a little more patient with six-year-olds." If you say that, then guess what? You were just disrespectful again. Now you owe him *another* apology, so you're no better off than when you first started the conversation. It's important that you listen to his response after you apologize and acknowledge that you *really* heard him. Sometimes I repeat what I heard him say. You might wrap up by saying, "Yeah, I'm really sorry about that," but don't offer anything more about this topic.

In some cases, not responding may require putting large quantities of duct tape over your mouth. Do whatever it takes.

Emily struggled when I first suggested that she apologize for being disrespectful to her husband, Tim, after she had criticized his efforts to install a new light fixture in the kitchen. She explained, "He was being so illogical, standing on a chair that was about to topple over, and balancing himself with one foot on the new kitchen table that we had just stained with a beautiful new finish. All he needed to do was walk into the garage and get the stepladder and I told him so. Why then do I have to apologize for being disrespectful when he was being lazy and careless of our new table?"

Emily had a point.

But criticizing Tim and using a condescending tone only made their Saturday tense. He resisted getting the stepladder because he didn't want to be controlled. And once he felt her grip, he certainly didn't feel affectionate towards her. Needless to say, he wasn't in the mood for laughter or a long conversation, or quiet snuggling on the couch—the small Saturday afternoon things that foster big feelings of closeness.

I encouraged Emily to apologize just this once. According to her, she mumbled the dreaded word when she delivered her line, "I apologize for being disrespectful when I criticized the way you put in the light fixture." Emily's tone didn't matter. Her husband had a tender smile for her when he said, "I love seeing this side of you."

Cathy's husband hung the welcome mat up to dry by putting nails in it. "Now there are holes in my welcome mat," she complained. "Are you saying I shouldn't even tell him my opinion about that?" Since there's no respectful way to tell your husband that he did something you consider stupid, a surrendered wife would simply not say anything. Instead, she would keep in mind, as Cathy did, that this is a man who works hard to support the family, who will bring her a glass of water in bed, who plays with the baby so she can take long bubble baths, and makes her laugh. In the great scheme of things, a couple of holes in the welcome mat are not a big deal.

Collette was in a similar situation when her husband accidentally threw out one of her toddler's favorite toys. "I'm the one who has to pay for this with my son," she told me. "My husband will be at work when the temper tantrum starts this afternoon. I'm so angry, I could just spit!"

This husband she was thinking of spitting on also had some redeeming qualities. He had agreed to raise their son in her faith and not his, made a concerted effort to get along well with her family, and worked so that she could stay home with their child. After some contemplation, Collette realized it was not in her best interest to bring up the toy and instead vented to friends about his transgression. As a result, she avoided a night of bickering followed by silence. You know what else she avoided? A baby crying in reaction to hearing his parents fight—and a night of sleeping stiffly on her side of the bed. So, refraining from making a critical comment wasn't such a big sacrifice after all.

Learning to treat my husband with respect seemed impossible to me at first because I was so convinced that I was superior to him, but the rewards were well worth it and quickly reinforced my new behavior. I found dignity and self-respect, not to mention harmony, better intimacy, and a husband who adores me. The women I know who have decided to make this change, however imperfectly, find the same is true for them. If we can do it, so can you.

Your husband will adore you for it.

2

GIVE UP CONTROL
TO HAVE MORE POWER

> *"When a man does not feel loved just the way he is, he will either consciously or unconsciously repeat the behavior that is not being accepted. He feels an inner compulsion to repeat the behavior until he feels loved and accepted."*
> — JOHN GRAY

Stop telling your husband what to do, what to wear, what to say and how to do things, even if you think you're helping. As much as possible, mind your own business. Recognize that when your urge to control him comes up, you may be feeling fear that isn't appropriate to the situation.

Write down five situations where you have been controlling with your husband recently. For each situation, ask yourself what it was you were afraid would happen? Was your fear realistic? What was the worst-case scenario? Did needing to control the situation justify losing intimacy with your husband? Practice facing your fear and relinquishing control of your husband to create room for intimacy, and to become the best person you can be.

*J*ust underneath the urge to control is fear—big fear. I'd go so far as to call it terror. But what is it we're so afraid of?

Many women are terrified that their husbands won't know how to perform everyday duties properly when left to their own devices. These women are convinced that their husbands are so inept that they are a perpetual threat to the whole family's well being—unless the wives step in. Everyday I see exhausted, exasperated women who insist that unless they manage how their husband does everything—be it parenting, tracking the finances, performing in his job, or even brushing his teeth—things will fall apart.

Some women say they are afraid to leave the children with their own father while they go out because they're "sure" he won't bother to make them a proper dinner or put them to bed on time or check to see that their homework is completed. Others doubt their husbands' ability to plan an enjoyable evening out or to negotiate a good deal on a car. I have to smile when women tell me these kinds of concerns, because I remember not too long ago, I thought the same way. Now I challenge those familiar fallacies by asking "Do you think he would let the kids starve? Do you think you'll go bankrupt buying a minivan?"

As irrational as it sounds, the short answer to those questions is, "Yes."

Women feel the need to control because they fear that if they don't take matters into their own hands, their needs will go unmet.

It is possible that your husband is thoughtless or inept, but until you give him your complete trust over a sustained period of time, you can't be sure. Chances are he is a great guy who spends most of his time defending himself against your criticism. Until you stop trying to run his life, you'll never know what it's truly like to be married to your husband. I am *not* saying that you are the cause of your husband's shortcomings. Your husband is always completely responsible for his own actions. If he is a poor father or neglects his family, that is not his wife's fault. At the same time, if you are nagging, undermining, criticizing, or disrespecting him, you are crushing his confidence, intellect, and potential—both emotionally and financially.

The "No-Control" Date

"*I have not ceased being fearful, but I have ceased to let fear control me. I have accepted fear as a part of life, specifically the fear of change, the fear of the unknown, and I have gone ahead despite the pounding in the heart that says: turn back, turn back, you'll die if you venture too far.*"

— ERICA JONG

My own terror was so strong that I had great difficulty going with my husband on what we called the "no-control date." My therapist encouraged me to experiment with the concept of trusting my husband by agreeing to go on a date where he made all the decisions—just for one night. On this particular date, he was to tell me how to dress and what time to be ready. He would also drive, pick a restaurant, order for me, pay, and plan any other activities for this one evening. This would give me the opportunity to relax and practice trusting him to be in charge for a change.

It would also prove that despite my superiority complex, my

husband would indeed give me what I needed and wanted, right down to ordering my favorite meal for dinner. Agreeing to do this exercise meant I would deliberately be vulnerable—a state that I would normally do anything to avoid.

The therapist must have known that I would have trouble letting go when she assigned the exercise. She must have realized that my habit of calling all the shots would be hard to turn off, even for one night, and that it would be impossible to sit with my fear.

I did so poorly with this experiment that by the time we were backing out of the driveway, I had already figured out where John was taking me and I was telling him the best way to get there. At the restaurant, I told him where to park and squirmed anxiously in my chair as he ordered the dinner I had strategically mentioned appealed to me.

The service that night was abominable. The food took far too long and the waitress ignored us. I told my husband I would ask to speak to the manager and get him to give us our dinners for free because of the extraordinary wait. John assured me we were in no hurry and that he was happy to pay for the dinner. He said he was just enjoying the opportunity to sit and talk with me!

I was beside myself with anxiety. When we finally left the restaurant, I begged him to please take me home (instead of to the movies as he had planned) because I was so distressed. But why was I terrified to be out on a date with my husband? It made no sense!

At no point during the evening was I in any danger of being hurt, embarrassed, bored, deprived, or even having to eat something I didn't like. But to see how I acted, you might have thought I was going before a firing squad. That's how big my fear was.

In reality, my terror had nothing to do with him. I was with a man who knows me well and wants me to be happy. In fact, I was terrified of being out of control long before I met him.

Dominating a situation, however ungraciously, somehow made me feel grounded and safe in an unpredictable world. Finally, as I tried to give up my unpleasant behavior, I learned to dig a little deeper when my urge to control came up and simply say that I was afraid. Unfortunately, this was only a little better in terms of healing my relationship and restoring intimacy. It wasn't until I discovered my "trust muscles"—and started exercising them—that I started to get the connection I'd always wanted.

When Amy talked about her husband, she explained to me that there is always a reason she needs to control his actions. The reason he should eat less red meat is because it's better for his health. The reason he should take one route to the city and not the other is because it would save time and hassle. The reason he should install the curtains her way is because it's more efficient.

The real "reason" Amy can't stop controlling her husband is because she's terrified that if she relinquishes even the tiniest bit of control for a minute, she will lose something precious to her. In this case, she fears losing her husband to heart disease, or having to wait for him because he doesn't know the efficient way to get to work or fix up the house. Like most controlling people, Amy is very bright, and has a distinct set of ideas about what should happen, and how.

Telling her husband how to do things provides her with the illusion of safety, but what she has also done is signaled to him that she doesn't trust him.

The Seven Habits of a Highly Effective Shrew

~

> *"If a relationship is to evolve, it must go through*
> *a series of endings."*
> — Lisa Moriyama

There are many ways to be controlling, and I've probably tried them all.

Years ago my husband told me a story about a couple he observed while waiting his turn for a haircut that illustrated just how controlling I could be. While the barber was trying his best to cut the man's hair, his wife was standing by giving the barber explicit instructions. "Not too short in the back," she told him, "and make sure it doesn't stick out on the top!"

Several other men were waiting for haircuts as well, and when the barber finished and the couple left, everyone sighed with relief. My husband got in the chair next and told the barber, "My wife couldn't be here today, so you're on your own."

Even though I recognized myself in this story, I wasn't able to change my seven shrewish habits. I couldn't seem to keep from (1) talking on my husband's behalf and making decisions for him. I told myself that it was a good thing I did, or he would be a mess. Sometimes I would resist uttering criticisms, but (2) give my husband a disapproving look. This seemed less offensive to me, but not to him. When I tried to stop giving him "the look," I started (3) asking questions that seemed innocent enough but clearly conveyed my disapproval. (i.e., You're going to wear *that?*) I would (4) try to explain to my husband what I would do if I were in his situation, hoping that he would do what I thought he should. I've made (5) countless unsolicited suggestions, (6) gasped in the car while he was driving, and (7) frowned at the lettuce he bought, all in the desperate, futile attempt to modify his actions.

None of those tactics got me the intimacy I craved. Instead, they annoyed my husband. It seemed like John was always waiting for me to decide what we should do, and then dragging his feet once I did. I might have been getting some things done my way, but now John was dependent on me. I was exhausted from doing everything and lonely because I was doing it all by myself.

If your husband doesn't speak up when he gets a haircut or doesn't pay attention to the route when he's driving, it could be because he's always expecting you to pipe up. If you jump in and tell him what to do because you think he can't figure it out, you are encouraging him to cruise while you maneuver. If he hasn't already, he will lose the impetus to do things for himself because he knows that his wife-crutch is always there.

You might argue that it's a two-way street. You could say, as I have before, that if he would stop being so obnoxious or lazy, you wouldn't have to get after him and "help."

Perhaps you think someone should write a book for men explaining how they can be more responsible husbands.

Perhaps someone should.

But you couldn't make your husband read it, or do what it says. So your only chance of improving your marriage is to change your behavior. I'm reminded of the Serenity Prayer:

God, grant me the serenity to accept the things I cannot change [like my husband]

The courage to change the things I can [like myself]

And the wisdom to know the difference [between him and me].

Responding to His Crazy Ideas

-𓂃𓇬

> *He early on let her know who is the boss. He looked her*
> *right in the eye and clearly said, "You're the boss."*
> — Anonymous

One of the most difficult things about relinquishing control is that we don't always *know* when we're being controlling.

Letting your husband know how little regard you have for his ideas is the most dangerous and subtle form of control. When you squash your husband's ideas you are telling him you don't trust him. Without trust there can be no intimacy. Therefore, one of the keys to relinquishing control is to respect your husband's thinking.

Your husband may make a pronouncement that sounds silly. He's human and he deserves the space to think about things, concoct crazy schemes, and make mistakes, just as you do. We all need the freedom to muse out loud about whatever it is we're thinking. So, the first step in respecting your husband's thinking is to let him think out loud without criticizing, laughing at, dismissing, or insulting him.

Instead, say with as much kindness and sincerity as you can muster, "Whatever you think" when he is telling you his ideas. For instance, if he comes up with a nutty thought that he should change jobs, and this strikes terror in your heart, you say, "Whatever you think." If he says he thinks the kids should learn how to ski, and this sounds dangerous to you, say, "Whatever you think." If he says he thinks the two of you should go out to dinner, and you think you should save money and eat at home, say, "Whatever you think."

Even if you think what he's saying is lunacy, respond by reminding him that you respect what he thinks. Practice saying, "Whatever you think" repeatedly because it's difficult to form those words when you really need them most. For best results, use this phrase exactly like you see it here. I've heard variations on this phrase such as "It's up to you," "What do you think?" "That's for you to decide" and "Whatever you want," but none of these communicates both implicit trust in his thinking and a healthy detachment from his problems as well as "Whatever you think."

Of course, this phrase also implies that you agree with whatever he thinks, which means you're going to end up agreeing to a lot of things that you never would have before. It's not as dangerous as it sounds—all you're really doing is allowing your man to be himself.

Sometimes your husband's ideas will materialize and sometimes they won't. But if you trust him—and respect his ideas rather than trying to control what actually comes to fruition—I guarantee that you will be one step closer to fostering intimacy with your husband. He may lose money. He may make you late. The kids might get bruised knees. He may make a mess, or lose his job or let the bills go so long that the water gets turned off.

None of those situations is permanent, none of them is life threatening, and all of them are part of being human. They can certainly put a strain on your marriage, but they don't have to. You have the power to choose whether you fight about something for days or laugh about it for years.

Many of us harbor the illusion that when we reject disagreeable thoughts and ideas immediately, those thoughts die and never materialize into actions with unpleasant consequences. We believe that we won't have to deal with the financial uncertainty of a job change if we tell him it's not a good idea. We think we won't have to be afraid for our children's safety if we dismiss his idea of teaching them to ski. We won't have to watch our husband suffer and curse while repairing the plumbing himself if we give him "the look" that lets him we know we don't think he can do it.

The problem is that when your squash your husband's ideas, you kill his spirit. When you disrespect your husband's thinking, he feels rejected. You give him no choice but to believe that you already know what's best and have complete veto power. You are letting him know who is in charge: you. He has that recurring thought, "Why bother?" And you are left with feeling tired from shouldering all the responsibility.

But this vicious circle can be interrupted. If you respond to your husband's ideas with trust, he will feel a new level of responsibility. If he says he can fix the plumbing himself, and you say, "whatever you think," he will feel the full weight of the task on his shoulders and probably even some fear. He will think more seriously about the task before deciding whether he wants to take it on.

THE MAGIC OF GRATITUDE

> *"Try to want what you have, instead of spending your strength trying to get what you want."*
> —ABRAHAM L. FEINBERG

*B*ut what if he says or does something really stupid, then what do I do?"

"But what if I completely disagree with him?"

"But what if I know I'm right and he's wrong?"

If you're like me, you probably think that these are the situations in which you can make an exception and maintain control.

Nope.

Instead, they are the times when you especially need to surrender.

When you find yourself desperate to steer your husband's actions, consider your choices: Either you hold your tongue and preserve harmony or you speak critically and create a chasm of resentment and resistance. Once you speak the first note of discord he will distance himself from you. Contradicting is sure to exasperate him and cause a great divide. If you are condescending (and telling your husband what to do is always condescending), you will have to endure his aloofness and sulking afterwards.

If you keep quiet, keep breathing, and remind yourself that this too shall pass, the one stress you won't have is a marital problem. What a relief!

When your spouse appalls you, keep in mind that you married a capable, loyal, hard-working, dependable man. When things go wrong as a result of your husband's decisions, remember that he is learning. Next time, he'll probably invest more carefully or have the kids wear kneepads or hire a professional. If you don't make a big deal about his mistakes, he'll begin to take initiative in every area.

Isn't that what you've always wanted? Somebody who had his own ideas and acted on them?

The Distress Test

> *"We are most deeply asleep at the switch when we fancy we control any switches at all."*
> —Annie Dillard

The only time you might disagree with what your husband thinks is if he wants you to do something that would require you to sacrifice your emotional or physical well-being. If he thinks you should hike in the desert heat, and you know this will cost you dearly in terms of emotional balance and physical health, then you must simply say, "I can't." If your doctor prescribes medication that keeps you vital and your husband thinks you should give it up and try a homeopathic remedy, you can tell him that doesn't fit for you. If your husband thinks you should work full-time and you would be devastated to be away from your children for so long, then don't do it. Conversely, if your husband thinks you should be a full-time mom and you know it would drive you mad to be home all the time, then don't do that either.

The way to tell if a situation falls into this category is to ask yourself if you will feel serious physical or emotional distress as a result. If he thinks the two of you should go whaling in Greenland and it's not your favorite idea for a holiday, then you'd want to go along with your husband because there are no serious emotional or physical consequences. Do you see the difference? The holiday is not ideal for you, but it doesn't threaten your well-being. The key point is that you are not controlling him: You are looking at yourself and your own limitations.

Typically though, when a wife is surrendering, her husband doesn't ask her to do things that he suspects will make her uncomfortable or unhappy. A surrendered wife usually only needs to say what she wants or doesn't want to win her mate's agreement, because treating a man respectfully brings out his natural tendency to treasure his wife. When he realizes he has your full faith and trust, he will not want to let you down, and will feel a fierce responsibility to meet your expectations. In fact, chances are he'll take you somewhere besides Greenland on vacation if he knows you'd rather be in a bikini on deck.

The more you relinquish control and respect your husband's thinking, the more powerful and masculine he will feel. Your faith gives him added strength and reminds him who he is and that he wants to take care of you and ensure your delight.

If he feels disrespected, his natural instinct to provide, protect, and adore his wife is derailed. When a wife respects her husband, he naturally responds with more confidence in himself and gratitude for his wife. This makes him cherish her more, and spend more time and effort memorizing the things that make her happy.

BE THE VIP INSTEAD OF THE CHAUFFEUR

The scariest part about surrendering to your husband is that it may seem like you're never going to get your way, but just the opposite is true.

When you give up *unnecessary* control of things your husband does—how he drives, what he wears, what he does at work, how he loads the dishwasher—you actually gain power in the relationship and in your life. Doing all the work is not what makes you powerful—it's what makes you exhausted. On the other hand, relaxing and enjoying yourself while someone else takes care of things is a very powerful position to be in. Certainly the VIP who rides in the limousine is more powerful than the chauffeur who controls the vehicle. Here are two more situations that illustrate this idea:

Toni is overwhelmed with doing everything around the house, going to work, taking care of the kids, and trying to make ends meet when she pays the bills. She has to nag her husband to do things for her, but when he forgets, she frequently ends up doing them herself. Toni lets her husband know how everything should be done, but he can never seem to get it right. Although Toni doesn't realize it, her husband is on the verge of having an affair with a coworker who admires him.

Barbara is also busy taking care of kids, but her husband earns most of the income and pays all of the bills for the family, so she doesn't worry about that. She often asks her husband for help and relinquishes tasks that are stressful for her. Recently he attended a parent-teacher conference for their son (to relieve Barbara of the chore when she said she found the teacher contentious). Barbara rarely tells her husband what to do, but he is always thinking of things to please her. Although Barbara doesn't realize it, her husband is buying her a diamond anniversary ring.

Toni is staying in control of everything to avoid being a victim. Barbara is relinquishing control to her husband so she can relax more. Who do you think has the most power? Which one would you rather be?

PRESURRENDERING NEGOTIATIONS

> *"The only thing worse than a man you can't control is a man you can."*
> — MARGO KAUFMAN

*P*ut yourself in the room with the following conversations John and I had before I surrendered. Most of them took place in our living room at times when we could have been relaxing together, reading the paper or playing. Instead, this is how our discussions went:

EXAMPLE 1: GIFT FOR A FRIEND

HIM: I gotta get a present for Steve for Christmas.

ME: Do you have to? He didn't get you a present last year!

HIM: Well, I want to.

ME: We don't have much cash right now, so don't spend more than $20. Do you have to get him something?

HIM: Well . . . maybe something little.

ME: I know, what if I bake cookies and we give him some in a tin?

HIM: Yeah, okay.

ME: Let's do that.

EXAMPLE 2: PAINTING THE HOUSE

ME: We've got to get the house painted. I think we should get started on it today.

HIM: I don't think so. I hadn't really thought about it and I was going to do some other things today. Maybe we could do it next weekend.

ME: It's supposed to start raining next week. You never want to paint the house! What do you think the neighbors think of this place? It looks awful out there.

HIM: We'll wait until after next week then, but this really isn't a good time.

ME: Why not?

HIM: Because we have other things to do today.

ME: I'll paint it by myself then. I'll just do it myself.

HIM: Why can't you just wait?

ME: Because you never want to do it!

HIM: ArrrggghhhhHH!

EXAMPLE 3: CAR MAINTENANCE

HIM: The brakes are starting to go on the car, so I'm gonna take it in next week.

ME: Next week? Brakes are pretty serious, John. Don't you think you should take it in right away? You can't drive without brakes.

HIM: I don't have time right away. The brakes are good enough to last another week.

ME: Hmm. I think you should take it in right away. Why wait until next week?

HIM: I'm not going to have time right now.

ME: You need to make time for things like that.

HIM: There's just too much going on and it has to be next week.

ME: So are you going to take it in?

HIM: Next week!

ME: Maybe I can take it in for you.

HIM: Why don't you just put my head under the wheel and drive over it?

I had veto power over everything, but that also meant that now everything was under my jurisdiction. The responsibility that accompanied the control had me stressed out and utterly exhausted. For protection, my husband placed himself before the television.

POSTSURRENDERING CONVERSATIONS

Today, if I were to have those same conversations with my husband, they'd go something like this:

EXAMPLE 1: GIFT FOR A FRIEND

> HIM: I gotta get a present for Steve for Christmas.
> ME: Okay.

John is in charge of the household finances, so I don't need to worry about what we can afford. I have my money, so this purchase will not affect me. Instead of discounting John's friends as I would have before, I honor them because I recognize that they offer him things that I can't, just as there are things I share only with my girlfriends. John enjoys giving gifts to me, and it also gives him pleasure to show his affection and appreciation to his friends. Finally, how ridiculous is it for me to pick a present for *his* friend? Don't answer that!

EXAMPLE 2: PAINTING THE HOUSE

> ME: I wish the outside of our house looked better. I want new paint. What do you think?
> HIM: I think we should go to the paint store, buy some paint, and start painting.

This is a real-life example! Notice that I just said what I wanted, not how it should happen. He could also have said, "Let's hire somebody to do it." Of course, he could have also said, "I think we should wait until spring and then paint it."

I would have gone along with either scenario because I'd rather not spend my energy trying to get John to do something he doesn't want to do. If we had painted the house when John didn't want to, I would have gotten my way, but it would have irritated John. Harmony and closeness are much greater gifts than having a house the neighbors admire for its fresh paint.

EXAMPLE 3: CAR MAINTENANCE

HIM: The brakes are starting to go on the car, so I'm going to take it in next week.

ME: Thank you for taking care of that.

Once again, I don't need to worry about what he's doing because I trust my husband to maintain the car without any input from me. After all, he was doing it long before he met me, and his method worked. Maybe he didn't do it the way I thought he should, but that didn't mean he was being irresponsible.

THE PATH TO INTIMACY, PASSION AND PEACE

*S*ome women worry that their husbands will be shocked and find them insincere when they say, "Whatever you think." But not surprisingly, most husbands are just so glad to be trusted that they don't want to ruin it by asking questions. Still, even if you're worried that your husband will doubt the new you, don't get into a long discussion trying to convince him that you really mean what you say. That just opens too many cans of worms. Rather, it's best to just reinforce the original message. You might say, "I'm sure you've got it handled," or "I'm just relieved that I don't have to think about it."

Along this path of respect, you will find peace, relief, joy, and passion that you will never find any other way.

3

KEEP SURRENDERING
A SECRET

> "Wisdom is divided into two parts: (a) having a great deal to
> say, and (b) not saying it."
> —Anonymous

Promise yourself that you will practice surrendering for
at least six months before you tell your husband about
being a surrendered wife. Instead of confiding in him, find
a girlfriend or two who will listen and support you in
your process.

*I*f you're like me, your first instinct will be to tell your husband everything you've learned about the practices of a surrendered wife. You might even be tempted to hand him this book. Instead, I urge you to *consider keeping this new information to yourself.* The idea of keeping secrets from your husband may sound counter to the whole concept of being intimate. After all, how can you expect to be truly connected and understand each other if you don't share all of your feelings?

Yet here are some of the things I've heard bright, thoughtful women say to their husbands when they're newly surrendered (I'm not making these up!):

"I'm supposed to start respecting you more, according to this book."

"This author says I shouldn't give you advice. I don't think that's right, do you?"

"I'm going to start surrendering because I'm sick of doing everything around here! Now you'll see what it's like to have to do some of the work."

"According to this book, I'm supposed to just keep my mouth shut when you do the dishes wrong/wear something that doesn't match/don't change the baby's diapers right."

"From now on, I'm going to appreciate your little gifts."

"I'm going to pretend I respect you and believe in you, even when I don't."

In each of these statements is an inherent criticism or controlling comment. Here's why they slip out: In the beginning, the anger, loneliness, depletion, and resentment you feel are prominent, and it's almost impossible to keep from expressing those feelings in a related conversation. However, doing so will do further damage to the intimacy in your relationship, which is discouraging when you're just starting out.

I don't know of any benefit in talking to your husband about surrendering. It's like visiting a bakery when you're just starting a new diet. If you aren't in the habit of passing up sweets yet, you might succumb to a chocolate éclair, thus setting yourself back before you've had a good start. Once you develop the *habit* of passing up pastries, however, that same visit to the bakery will be less challenging because you will have already practiced resisting temptation. Also, you have momentum, and that makes you stronger.

I'm making a special plea for your discretion in this matter because I've noticed a common tendency among wives to disregard this suggestion. Some women tell me that they know they aren't supposed to tell their husbands about surrendering, but their husband is different, or they themselves are different, or they always share everything with their husband.

One woman described a conversation where she told her husband about surrendering because she wanted him to know that it was hard for her to trust him because he had let her down so many times before. Ouch! She then went on to say that she felt better for having had this conversation even though she knew I advised against it. She probably did feel better in the short run. But telling her husband that he had let her down so many times before when she is trying to build trust and intimacy is the equivalent of consuming a big hunk of cheesecake at the onset of a diet— defeating!

No Trumpets Will Sound

⁂

> *"I often regret that I have spoken; never that I am silent."*
> — Publilius Syrus

*W*on't my husband know there's something going on?" women often ask me. Of course he will. Most husbands are acutely aware of their wife's moods and habits (even if they seem oblivious). Not only will your husband be pleasantly surprised to find that his wife is treating him respectfully, and that she seems more appreciative and happier, he will have a new, deep sense of peace because his entire day-to-day experience will be changed. In turn, he, too, will probably seem easier to live with because he won't be reacting to the tension and bickering that is usually present in your marriage.

Still, he's not likely to come out and ask you what you're up to. He's not going to present you with a gold medal, a blue ribbon, or even a necklace. The change is subtle, kind of like feeling better after a bad cold. You're healthy again, but you haven't changed so monumentally that people are coming up to you saying how lovely you look without puffy eyes and a red nose. You're just back to your old affable self.

Since surrendering to your husband is more about the absence of an old behavior, it's likely to take a while before your husband notices. Initially, he may be waiting for the other shoe to drop. Eventually, he will start to trust your new behavior.

There's another reason your husband probably won't ask you why you're behaving differently. If he's accustomed to waiting to find out what to do from you, he's going to get reacquainted with his own voice. This is the same voice that told him he was attracted to you, loved you, and wanted to marry you. Hearing it again for the first time in a long while may distract him altogether from what you're doing.

Surrendering to your husband is going to change your whole life, and it's going to change his too, but talking about it and doing it are not at all the same thing.

The New You Is the Real You

> *"You must be the change you wish to see in the world."*
> — Mahatma Gandhi

*W*hen Paula first surrendered she was feeling especially uncomfortable with "keeping secrets" from her husband although she was seeing remarkable changes in her marriage. I suggested that she plan to tell her husband what she was doing, but only after she'd been doing it for at least six months. She agreed, and when six months had passed, Paula had transformed. She no longer felt judgmental toward her husband, and she realized there really wasn't any secret to disclose. Her husband knew she had changed and didn't seem the least bit betrayed that she hadn't told him what she was doing sooner. He even knew it had something to do with being a surrendered wife, and which of her friends were involved in surrendering.

You may be tempted to ask your husband how he likes the "new you" or if he's noticed anything different lately. It's human to want some positive reinforcement. You do deserve pats on the back for having the courage to take this difficult journey. Lots of women will never find the strength to do what you're doing, so your perseverance is admirable. However, your husband is not the appropriate person to ask for such reinforcement. Although you are doing a lot of hard work, you can't really ask your husband to gush about how you haven't been controlling or rude to him in a while.

All you've done is come back to being your best self: the one who is good-natured and easy to please. The one who laughs easily and listens well. The one who is so thrilled to love and be loved by the man of her dreams.

4

TAKE CARE OF
YOURSELF FIRST

> *"To put the world right in order, we must first put the nation in order; to put the nation in order, we must first put the family in order; to put the family in order, we must first cultivate our personal life; we must first set our hearts right."*
> —CONFUCIUS

Surrendering takes patience and concentration, which are nearly impossible to conjure when you're fried and frazzled. Usually there's a direct connection between self-care and your level of tolerance for your husband.

Make one list of ten things that you like doing because they're fun, and a second list of ten things that you like doing because you feel good afterwards. Doing at least one or two things from each category everyday is a good rule of thumb. Consciously doing three things a day to care for yourself is a powerful way to guard against depletion.

When you find yourself losing patience with and interest in your husband, check to see if you've been neglecting your self-care.

The quickest way to rediscover your good-natured self is to practice good self-care. Without ongoing attention to your own pleasure and desires, life starts to look pretty grim, and just making it through the day seems like a big accomplishment. When you're using every last drop of energy to exist, there isn't any extra to put into an intimate, passionate relationship, which naturally requires some effort. So if you have none to give, you're giving your marriage absolutely no chance to thrive.

Imagine you're on a plane when the cabin pressure drops suddenly. The oxygen masks fall from the ceiling and in order to stay conscious, you have to put one on. But you're traveling with a child who will also need an oxygen mask.

Whose mask do you put on first?

If you attend to the child first and then pass out, it's unlikely that the child will be able to help you with yours. Therefore, it's critical that you take care of yourself first, then help the child.

The same is true with surrendering—always take care of yourself first. When a woman is particularly irritated at her husband's annoying habits, poor self-care is almost always the underlying reason. The minute you become sleep deprived, hungry, overwhelmed or just plain stressed out, you're not much good to anybody, including yourself. Once you're stretched beyond your limits, surrendering is nearly impossible. Surrendering means that you commit to being compassionate and understanding, which require patience and concentration. All of these qualities disappear when we feel run-down and anxious. The more well-rested, well-nourished and balanced you are in work, rest and play, the more sure-footed you will be on the high road of surrendering.

SIMPLE PLEASURES WILL HELP YOU SURRENDER

> *Forget not that the earth delights to feel your bare feet and*
> *the winds long to play with your hair.*
> — KAHLIL GIBRAN

So what does it look like to take care of yourself first? It means making sure that you don't work yourself into an exhausted frazzle. It also means finding the time to take a walk, indulge in a hot bath, or squeeze in a nap even if it seems that you have too much to do. It means valuing simple pleasures such as watching your favorite TV show. Without these simple "indulgences," which I actually think are necessary, everything—including marriage—seems hard. In general terms, it means honoring your female nature.

Unlike our work selves where we are always trying to get things done, at home, we don't have to accomplish something to have worth. When we feel self-confident and cherished, we have the dignity just to "be" and not necessarily "do." We might find nourishment in talking with other women, holding a baby or lounging on the deck with a good book and a glass of lemonade.

Sophie had done nothing but work, clean the house, chauffeur the kids from one activity to the next, and plan for a big party she was throwing on Saturday. At the end of the week, the dog wrestled with a skunk, and Sally just lost it. She came to me with a litany of complaints about her husband, Justin. He didn't make it to the cleaners when he said he would. His car was filthy. He left the fax machine on instead of the answering machine again.

Justin and Sophie have been our friends for years, and I know that she is a hard-working and kind woman and Justin is wonderful and adoring with only the usual number of human foibles. I could tell from Sophie's intolerance for his ordinary shortcomings that she must have been feeling spent, and I reminded her about self-care.

"Oh yeah," she said. "That's probably the problem. I haven't done anything nice for myself in so long I can't remember what it feels like."

No wonder Justin was getting on her nerves! Sophie was depleted. The next day at lunch she made it to the beach to read a book, bought a new welcome mat and gave herself a pedicure. For the next few days, she committed ahead of time to do at least three nice things for herself to restore her well-being. She scheduled her morning meetings for 10:00 instead of 9:00 and vowed to go for a walk to clear her head. She gave herself permission to get take-out for dinner so that she wasn't preoccupied with the planning, cooking, and cleaning of the big meal at night. She also decided to sleep in on Saturday morning instead of getting up early to run errands before her real weekend started. Allowing herself these small comforts each day helped Sophie feel less rushed and more relaxed and that improved her outlook on everything, including Justin, whose imperfections didn't seem quite as glaring.

CARVE OUT TIME FOR FUN AND PLEASURE

*"You yourself, as much as anybody in the entire universe,
deserve your love and affection."*
— BUDDHA

So how do you make sure you're doing enough self-care? There are two components that you need to be concerned about:

- Doing things that are fun.
- Doing things that make you feel better after you do them.

For me, going to a bookstore, watching my favorite TV show and having lunch with a friend constitute good self-care in the fun category. On the other hand, going to the gym always makes me feel healthy, and washing my windows gives me a Martha Stewart high. Cleaning my closets for Goodwill may not be so enjoyable while I'm knee deep in hangers and old, dusty dresses, but clearing clutter from my home tidies my head. I feel extra proud knowing that my old stuff may make another person's day as she discovers treasures among it.

Many of us are so busy, we don't even know what constitutes simple fun anymore, nor do we even recognize the little things we could do that would reward us with a feeling of accomplishment and its resulting self-esteem once they are completed. So, I recommend making one list of ten things that you like doing because they're fun, and a second list of ten things that you like doing—even if they take a little discipline—because you feel good afterwards. Then, try to do three things each day to ensure that your self-care is adequate. Eventually, this will become second nature.

Sometimes when I suggest that women do three things a day for themselves, they tell me there just isn't time in their schedule. If you're feeling the same way, ask yourself if you can let go of something to make room for *you*.

As Sophie tried to keep up her self-care, she came to the realization that she couldn't do it all—working full-time, taking care of the house, doing the grocery shopping, and looking after the dog allowed her no time for a regular regimen of self-care. She had a difficult decision to make: continue working full-time and feeling fried or cut back her work to only four days a week. This was a logical way to address her ongoing depletion, but at first it made her feel as if she was neglecting her work responsibilities.

Ultimately, when Sophie asked herself whether her first priority was to a big corporation or to herself and her marriage, the answer was a no-brainer.

Sophie knew that although her boss might raise an eyebrow at the idea of cutting back her work week, she was a valued employee who could still do her job well. In fact, knowing that she had fewer days in the office helped focus her, and she became more efficient at work. This is a little-known phenomenon among working women. Most people can do their jobs in less time. Think about whether this would work for you, too. Who says that we have to devote five sevenths of our time to someone else?

If you're thinking "That's nice for Sophie but it would never work at *my* company," think again. Just because you're the first at your company to ask for such a schedule doesn't mean the company won't accommodate you. It's scary to ask, but it's well worth it to restore your sanity.

If your life is arranged in such a way that there's no time for self-care, and you simply can't cut back at work, you're not off the hook with me. It's time to rearrange. Hire a housecleaner, or ask the babysitter to stay longer. Send your teenager with the new driver's license out to do the grocery shopping. Remember, until you get your self-care in, you're not going to be much fun to live with, and you certainly won't have the energy to surrender.

DON'T BEGRUDGE YOUR HUSBAND HIS SELF-CARE

"When nobody around you seems to measure up, it's time to check your yardstick."
— BILL LEMLEY

aith had trouble with self-care one week when her daughter was home sick from school. She felt trapped in the house by day, and neglected to make plans to get out of the house at night. Her husband stuck to his routine of working out two nights a week, but Faith did absolutely nothing for herself and so she started to resent that her husband had time to *himself*. Fortunately, she realized her own self-neglect was the problem, not her husband's good habits of exercising regularly. The next night she made plans to meet a friend for dinner, leaving her husband and kids to fend for themselves. Guess what? They ordered pizza and had a great time. Faith came back a new woman with a positive outlook on life.

Remember not to begrudge your husband taking care of himself. He deserves to enjoy a sense of peace and the desire for intimacy that flows from feeling relaxed and good about himself. As in Faith's situation, it wasn't inconsiderate of her husband to work out two nights a week, but it was self-neglect that Faith didn't do something for herself, too. It's easy to point the finger of blame at somebody who seems to be having more fun than we are when we're miserable.

You're Not the Only Responsible Adult in the Family

"Some women work so hard to make good husbands that they never manage to make good wives."

—Anonymous

When it comes to self-care, never ask for permission to do something. Simply announce what your plans are, as in "I'm going out with some girlfriends tonight." If you have children, leave it up to your husband to watch them or find other care for them. Don't say, "Will you watch the kids while I go out?" Just go, and trust him to take care of things or speak up if he needs something.

Obviously, you wouldn't want just to announce that you're going out on a night when you know he has plans because that would be inconsiderate. The point is not to inconvenience him or "let him have it" because he gets to go out and you don't. At the same time, don't assume that the kids are your sole responsibility when you have a perfectly capable man who is willing to share that responsibility with you.

When Donna started practicing good self-care by doing at least three things from her lists each day, she was amazed that no one in her family objected. "I thought I was being selfish at first," she admitted. In time she grew accustomed to having fun and feeling good every day, and even noticed a positive change at home. When she was happy and balanced, she was more available to support her family the way she always wanted to. What she considered "selfish" at first was actually a wonderful gift for the people she loved most.

5

EXPRESS
YOUR DESIRES

> *"The indispensable first step to getting the things you want out of life is this: decide what you want."*
> —BEN STEIN

Don't hesitate to tell your husband what you want, whether it's a vacation, new furniture, piano lessons for the kids, time to yourself, or even a baby. But make sure you are describing an end-result, not telling him how to do it.

When you tell your husband what you want without telling him when, why, and how you want him to get it— without controlling him—you are giving him a new opportunity to feel accomplished and proud about how happy he makes you. Letting him please you will make you feel adored and intimate.

*W*hen you treat yourself well by doing plenty of self-care, you also encourage everyone around you to treat you well, including your husband. Taking that one step further, the more you know what you want and say it out loud, the better your chances of getting it.

When you express a desire purely and simply, you're acknowledging and honoring your self and providing your husband with an opportunity—nothing more. By contrast, complaining that you don't have something is not only overbearing, it's downright unattractive.

Prior to surrendering, I used complaining and demanding to try to get my husband to do the dishes, which never worked. About a year ago I said, "I'd like to make us a nice dinner tonight, but it's going to make a mess and I don't want to do the dishes." He promptly offered to do them that night. In fact, he did them several times over the next week. Now he does them all the time and I never wash dishes. I started to wash them once many months ago and he said, "Thanks for doing the dishes for me."

Some of us have had the "I want" trained out of us. Maybe we were once told not to be so self centered, or to think of others who have less, or to be more practical. For instance, when a woman at the park told her preschool aged daughter that it was time to leave, the little girl said simply, "I don't want to go with you." The mother then responded by saying, "That's not very nice. Don't you like to be with your mother?" The mother twisted the daughter's statement of desire into a personal attack. She was unfortunately well on her way to training the "I want" out of her daughter.

Like the girl at the park, some of us were told it's not polite or considerate to express what we want, but that just isn't true.

Knowing what you want and being willing to express it are the purest ways to be true to yourself, which *is* a very attractive quality. The alternative to being direct about what we want is to be manipulative, which is totally unappealing. A third choice is to ignore our own desires, which means that we live without the things that would make us happiest, and suffer a corresponding drop in energy, vitality, and satisfaction with our lives. We also become resentful, and that's ugly.

Saying what you want means that you're aware of your feelings and desires and that you're willing to honor them. It means that you know that you deserve to have new things and things that you love. It means you don't have to waste energy thinking about how to get what you want by making it seem like it actually serves some other more noble purpose. You're not a martyr, and nobody has to guess what will please you. A woman who knows and respects herself simply says to her husband, "I want."

WHY MEN GO TO THE STORE FOR TAMPONS

If there hadn't been women we'd still be squatting in a cave eating raw meat, because we made civilization in order to impress our girlfriends.
—ORSON WELLES

It may not seem like it, but your husband wants to shower you with things that you love. As long as he knows you respect him, all you have to do is tell him what you want or don't want, as in "I want a cat" or "I want to send the kids to summer camp" or "I don't want to move." Whenever he can, the husband of a surrendered wife will gladly respond to these words because one of his foremost goals is to make his wife happy. If you don't believe me on that point, ask any married man you know how important it is that his wife is happy. I've asked hundreds of men this question, and their answers were always things like "Imperative," "Critical," and "It's everything."

Whenever I think about the men I know who will hold their wife's purse while she's in the fitting room, give up their jackets because she's cold, or run to the store for a box of tampons, I'm reminded of what great lengths men will go to for our happiness. On top of that, you see men moving their families across the country to be near her parents, commuting to work every day so she can live in a bigger house, and driving an old car so she can have the new one. Could their priorities be any more obvious?

Still, we have a tendency to ignore the fact that our husbands want to make us happy and to believe that saying what we want is poor form. Sometimes we try to make our men guess what we want so we don't have to acknowledge our own desires. To get a sense of what that's like, imagine a server at a restaurant comes to take your order, and instead of telling her what you want, you say, "I think you know," or "Can't you see I'm hungry?" At best, the server could suggest that you order the special, or she could choose something off the menu at random and bring it to you. Chances are slim that your dinner would be what you want.

Asking your husband to guess what you want is just one of the ways we try to avoid expressing our desires because we are uncomfortable admitting that we want something. Here are some of the other frustrating habits we have that prevent us from getting the desires of our hearts.

Stop Telling Him How to Get You What You Want

As I've said, trying to tell your husband how to do something is highly ineffective. Still, it's not unusual for women to try to get what they want by giving their husbands instructions about *how* to get it—as if he wouldn't otherwise know that there's such a thing as a florist or a mall nearby.

This doesn't work because when a husband feels controlled or disrespected, he gets worn down and lethargic. He reacts with stinginess and distances himself because he's lost the motivation to be generous. If you suspect your husband is stingy, it could be that he's been so preoccupied with defending himself and avoiding your criticism that he hasn't had the energy to focus on doing things to please you. If you excuse yourself from having to respect him because he seems so unkind and selfish, he will probably continue to withhold, and the two of you will be locked in a permanent standoff.

Let's go back into the restaurant for a minute to illustrate this point. The server wants to take your order, but instead of telling her what you want—say the apricot chicken—you begin telling her how to prepare it. You describe how to clean the chicken properly, then how to season it, and how much of each ingredient to use. You tell her how to cook it, and for how long, and how to garnish it so it will be appetizing. Naturally, the restaurant staff would find you pretty irritating. Even if they did follow your instructions, they'd probably also take a nice long cigarette break before they brought your food to the table because nobody wants to be told how to do his job.

Fortunately, most of us go into a restaurant and order a meal without telling the server how to make it. This works beautifully. The server gives the order to the cook, who prepares the dish, which arrives at our table. Everybody is happy.

Although I don't think of my husband as a server whose sole job is to fill my orders, this same system works very well in my marriage. If I tell my husband I want something, he works to get it for me as best he can.

If you think your happiness is a low priority for your husband, you're dead wrong. He's probably just responding defensively to you telling him how to do what you want him to do.

Once you are respecting him most of the time, his natural gratitude and desire to please you will surface, so start telling him what you want. Tell him in a way that is respectful and self-honoring by refraining from saying anything that could—even in the slightest way—be construed as controlling *how* he pleases you.

Just state your desire, and let him figure out the rest. When you say to your husband, "I want a new dress," or "I want another baby," or "I want a bigger house," you are giving him a new opportunity to feel accomplished and proud about how happy he makes you. In return, you do feel happy and taken care of, and both of you appreciate that.

Notice, however, that these examples are all end-results. Expressing the desire for a new dress is very different from telling him to go to the department store and buy you a blue dress for your birthday. Saying you want another baby is far different from telling him he needs to wear looser underwear to keep his sperm count up. Saying you want a bigger house is a lot different than telling him to ask for a raise so the two of you can afford one.

Do you see the difference? I'm suggesting that you tell him the end-result, but not specify *how* it happens.

Stop Telling Him Why He Should Get You What You Want

Another common technique that women use to try to motivate their husbands to do what they want is giving them lengthy explanations to justify their demands. As you can imagine, this approach is also highly ineffective.

Just as you would tell the server at a restaurant what you want without a long song and dance about how hungry you are because you haven't eaten all day, there's no need to elaborate about why you want what you want.

It's not necessary to say, "I want the apricot chicken because chicken is not as fatty as beef, and I like chicken with a sweet sauce on it and I've had the chicken here before and it's not too dry." Nor do you need to say, "I want to get a new dress because all of my old ones are worn out, and it's been three years since I bought anything new for myself, and I saved $40 on groceries with coupons last month." Although you're just adding explanations, they sound dangerously like complaints, which automatically put him on the defensive and may even cause him to tune out. The subtext of your message is "You never think I deserve anything, but I am going to tell you why you're wrong."

Telling your husband what you want isn't a play for power or a forum for testing how well he responds to your demands. Rather, it is a way for both of you to feel pleased. Saying, "I want a bigger house" is not the same as saying, "I want a new house because this one is so small it is absolutely driving me nuts! I'm sick of having to live in such cramped quarters. Plus, I think the neighborhood is going downhill. . . ."

Stop Making Demands

Many wives make demands, which cause terrible resentment. Saying, "You should buy me that necklace in the window at Tiffany's" is a demand. Any sentence that starts with "You should . . .", "Why don't you?" or "I want you to . . ." is automatically a demand because it's a request expressed with a sense of control.

When you demand something of your husband, you're still controlling him, still acting like his mother, and he will still resist being told what to do. Making a demand tends to raise his ire and actually push him away from getting you what you want.

Before you tell him what it is you want, think about it carefully and make sure that you are specific about the end result you have in mind. Expressing what you want is about letting your husband know what it is that you need and like, which is completely reasonable.

You are imparting information about yourself—not activating your control clutches. There's also no need to make requests—which can be perceived as demands—because your husband will want to give you what he knows you want.

In the movie *Phenomenon,* John Travolta's character visits a woman who lives on the outskirts of town, and gives her two kids a ride home along the way. When he gets there, she asks him what a man who drops in and brings her kids home is expecting—to be served dinner? Travolta responds by saying, "Not expecting, just hoping."

She served him dinner.

As you express your desires, be sure that you are not expecting, just hoping. As long as you do that, you are free to want absolutely everything in the world! Most women do. Don't be afraid to express your pure desire for something you want but fear your husband can't afford. You're not making a demand—but you are giving him the opportunity to surprise and please you.

Stop Asking for Permission or Agreement

Sometimes it's tempting to soften your desires by *asking* your husband for something instead of just saying you want it. This may sound odd, but I notice women express themselves in questions all the time. I did it not long ago when a friend was over. The windows were open in the living room, and as I jumped up to close them, instead of saying, "I'm cold" I said, "Aren't you cold? I'm going to close these." As it turns out she wasn't cold. She also didn't mind my closing the windows, but it had nothing to do with her desires. I was the one who wanted to warm up, but I tried to win her agreement to make myself feel less selfish.

One woman was disappointed when her husband refused her after she asked, "Can we take the kids for pizza tonight?" Again, she didn't come out and state her desire. She probably felt like she did, but instead, she asked him for something, as if he were Santa Claus, or her dad. Since he said, "No, not tonight," he was the bad guy.

By contrast, if this woman had said, "I want to go out for pizza with the kids tonight," as a statement, she would not have put any demands on him, but she would have given him the opportunity to make her happy.

Take ownership of your own desires by making a statement (as opposed to asking a question) that starts with "I want" or "I don't want."

Stop Projecting Your Desires

Sometimes we try to project our desires onto our husbands so that we don't seem to want so much. Have you ever said something like, "Don't you want to see the Grand Canyon this summer?" or "Don't you think it would be great to have a swimming pool?" I have. Then, when my husband says he doesn't feel strongly about seeing the Grand Canyon or getting a swimming pool, I'm compelled to argue with him about why he doesn't want what I want. Then he gets exasperated and just agrees with me to keep the peace. But I don't just want him to comply; I want him to feel the same way I do, even when he doesn't.

I find it's much easier to take ownership of my desires by saying, "I want to see the Grand Canyon this summer," or "I want to have a swimming pool."

A variation on this theme is using the word "we" when what you really mean is "I." Whenever you find yourself using the word "we" with your husband, chances are you're trying to distance yourself from your own desire.

When my husband hears me saying that "we" should do this or that, he immediately sees that I'm speaking for him out of a need to control. He doesn't care about things that "we" want. He cares about things that *I* want.

Instead of saying "we need to get the kids piano lessons" or "we need new miniblinds," try to say "I want to get the kids piano lessons" and "I want new miniblinds."

IF YOU DON'T ADMIT YOU WANT SOMETHING, YOU WON'T GET IT

"The stoical scheme of supplying our wants by lopping off our desires, is like cutting off our feet when we want shoes."
— JONATHAN SWIFT

About six years ago, I wanted to buy a new house in the worst way, but I thought we couldn't afford it. We had poor credit, a condo that was worth far less than we owed on it and no down payment. Still, I told my husband my desire. We looked at houses almost every weekend, and I hoped that somehow we'd find a way to buy one.

One rainy night my husband and I went to see a house that was advertised in the paper as "For Sale by Owner." The neighborhood was pleasant, but the house looked spooky, with dead trees in the yard and bars on all the windows. I was sure this could not be our house, but my husband saw immediately that it was. A few months later, we had sold our condo and bought the spooky house from the owner by assuming his loan. We got in without a credit check or a down payment, and sold the condo for the amount we owed on it, despite my belief that this was not possible. We took the bars off the windows and removed the dead trees and six years later I still love living in our beautiful four-bedroom house.

If John hadn't known what I wanted, he wouldn't have insisted on getting the house with the great potential, which I would have walked away from. Often you get what you want in a way that's not what you imagined.

The same thing happened with a friend of mine, who wanted carpet in her garage, where her toddler spent much of his time playing. She knew it wasn't in the financial plan, but she still let her husband know she wanted it. The next week he came home with a roll of carpet just the right size for the garage. A client had been putting in new carpet and had this extra to give to her husband for free.

A realtor told me the story of making a verbal offer on a million-dollar house on behalf of a client. As a joke he added, "and that price includes the Mercedes in the garage!" The sellers didn't realize he was joking, and when they accepted the offer, they agreed that the Mercedes would be part of the deal.

If I hadn't told my husband I wanted a house, he might not have persuaded me to buy the one we have now. If my friend hadn't told her husband she wanted carpet, he might have turned down his client's gift. If the realtor hadn't said the buyers wanted the Mercedes, they wouldn't have gotten it.

See how important it is to say what you want?

There's one more benefit to expressing your desires: A woman who is clear about what she wants also gives her husband an added gift. Her husband is confident that she wants him.

6

RELINQUISH THE CHORE
OF MANAGING THE FINANCES

> *"There is no security in this life. There is only opportunity."*
> —Douglas MacArthur

For greatest intimacy and less stress, let your husband handle the finances. Before you talk to him about it, read this chapter thoroughly and then go back and follow each of the steps.

If you're thinking you'll surrender in every way except financially, think again. You will miss out on some of the greatest benefits of surrendering if you skip this part.

At first, surrendering control of the finances seemed suicidal to me. I believed that if I didn't police the money that was coming in and going out of our bank account, my husband would spend it, well, wrong. He might buy a new guitar every month instead of saving for retirement. Maybe he would complain that I spent too much money on clothes. I worried that there wouldn't be enough for me, that I would have to go without.

My fixation on our finances exhausted me. I made budgets and put everything into the computer, but things never seemed to go as I planned. We always made less money or had more expenses or just spent too much. Although I was controlling the ebb and flow, I blamed John and resented that I had the unsavory job of paying the bills.

Finally there was a day when I was just too tired to do it anymore. The sight of the finance software and the pile of bills gave me a knot in my stomach. I was depleted. I could no longer do this miserable task, and so I just stopped. I told John I couldn't pay our bills anymore. I had *threatened* to do that before, but I never really meant it. I don't think he believed me at first, but this time I was serious. I finally let go.

When you let go of managing the finances, you'll also be letting go of the burden of that particular chore. Paying bills, balancing bank accounts, and worrying about whether there will be enough money to pay the mortgage—or just go out for dinner—is stressful. When you give up that responsibility, you also leave behind the anxiety and worry that comes with being the family banker.

The hardest part of relinquishing the finances was that I felt so vulnerable to John. When I considered whether it was worse to have the stress of the finances or to be that vulnerable, I had to keep reminding myself that the former has the added benefit of fostering intimacy.

Giving up control of the money is scary because often we see money as giving us a sense of security. If there's enough money—and we know where it is—we can assure ourselves that we will always be comfortable, that we can handle any emergency, that we can pay for any services—whether it's a haircut or a divorce attorney. So, what happens when you give up control of the finances? You are in the most vulnerable position of all because you now have to depend on your husband to keep you safe and comfortable. The result? You will have to trust him with all your might.

Here's why this topic is so loaded:

Money is about power. As a controlling wife, I saw our joint checking account as something I absolutely needed to oversee. If you are primarily responsible for paying the bills in your household, you have the power of spending money according to the right priorities—yours. That means your husband has no power—he is "impotent"—over how the money is spent in his family. Don't think this doesn't impact his view of himself.

Money is about worth. Not just worth in terms of dollars, but the really valuable kind—self-worth. When a man is responsible for how the family's income is divvied up, he has a stronger sense of his own worth. He takes more pride in providing for his family because he sees a direct relationship between what he earns and what he can provide for his family.

Money is about intimacy. For a man, there's nothing more conducive to intimacy than feeling proud and masculine. He'll never feel that more strongly than when he is protecting and supporting his family (if you don't have children, you are his family) by spending, saving, and investing. Therefore, when you give control of the finances to your husband, you take a powerful stride toward being more intimate with him.

As with other aspects of surrendering to your husband, relinquishing control of the finances is not a good idea for women whose husbands have an active addiction, such as alcoholism or gambling, are chronically unfaithful or physically abusive. If you're still uncertain whether your husband falls into one of these categories, *do not proceed with surrendering.* Instead, seek the help of a therapist or support group and determine whether you are with a safe man before you go any further.

If your husband already handles the financial affairs, I applaud your faith and ability to trust that you will be taken care of and would bet that you are already enjoying a degree of intimacy that many women have never experienced. However, I still encourage you to read this chapter to check for ways that you might still be subtly controlling with money.

THIS IS NOT FINANCIAL SUICIDE

Surrendering the financial control is essential for intimacy even if:

- You've maintained separate accounts for years and it's working just fine.
- You make more money than he does.
- You fear he'll bounce checks, or spend unwisely.
- You think you'll have less money for yourself.

If you're thinking it's about time you threw out this book right about now, take a deep breath and keep reading. If you're afraid of feeling powerless over your own hard-earned income, keep in mind that control is not the same as power. You are still going to have all the same spending power you've always had—without the hassle of doing the bookkeeping. You'll simply tell your husband what you need. No more calling the bank, balancing statements, or fretting about unexpected expenses. That's less stress—not less power.

THE THREE MIRACLES TO EXPECT

> *"There is no wealth but life."*
> —JOHN RUSKIN

The unromantic mother/son dynamic (where you tell your husband how much he can spend or what he can buy) is the first thing to go when you let him manage the finances. Remember: Men are not attracted to their mothers. The other changes that came about when I surrendered the finances were astounding. Not only was I reenergized when I stopped nagging and worrying, but there were miracles that I hadn't experienced since those glory days when John and I were dating:

1. The miracle of perpetual dating:

Remember when you and your husband first met and you basked in the feeling of being taken care of every time he paid the dinner bill, bought the movie tickets, or financed a trip? Why should that warm feeling disappear after years of marriage? When your husband manages the finances, you may feel vulnerable, yes, but you will also feel protected and looked after.

Perpetual dating literally means returning to the roles each of you played during your courtship. Remember how much fun that was? Let him open the door for you. Order what appeals to you instead of trying to keep the price down. Don't begrudge him spending money on his soda. Thank him for dinner, and tell him how much you enjoyed being with him. Let him take you out the way he used to. Or, if he didn't take you out in the beginning, let him start doing it now. You deserve it.

2. *The miracle of increased generosity:*

When husbands manage the money, they tend to be much more generous with their wives than the wives were with themselves. Perhaps it's because we're just trying to be practical and spend less to put a little more into savings or pay off debt or swing a room addition for the house. We know we can get by with the shoes we have. But to our husbands, giving us things above and beyond what we need is a joy, so they surprise and spoil us.

When we slice and dice the family income, we rob them of the joy of giving. No matter how successful he is, he feels like a little worker bee, passively providing for his family. Instead of showering his wife with gifts, he simply puts a roof over her head, food on the table, and clothes on her back. By contrast, when your husband controls the finances, he is in the position to give you gifts every day. If you're concerned that he'll forget or one day deny you your gifts, don't worry. That would be letting down the person who means the most to him in the world, and more than anything, men love the pride that comes with providing for and treating their wives. That delicious feeling of self-worth makes him feel masculine—and that's a wonderful jumping off point for intimacy.

3. *The miracle of greater prosperity:*

When you are in charge of the balances, your husband has no relationship to the money he earns. He is removed from any incentive to increase his income because he has little influence over how the money's spent.

When husbands have an immediate relationship with the finances, they feel the urgency to keep the coffers full and to earn more and provide well. Men have a clearer sense of where the money's going and how much extra (or deficit) is left after the bills are paid when they have a firsthand account of the family's monetary needs.

Furthermore, if he's had to accommodate your tendency to control everything—from when he goes to the doctor and dentist to how much money he spends—he has felt demeaned on some level, even if he hasn't expressed it. If you've long suspected that your husband could be making more money or doing more with his talents, you're probably right. Once he feels respected at home, his self-esteem increases, making him much more powerful at work. If the woman who knows him better than anyone else thinks he is sharp enough to handle the finances for the whole family and thanks him for doing such a good job, then he will start to believe that he is indeed smart and capable.

It makes sense if you think about it. The more you feel you're worth, the more likely you are to prosper. For instance:

- Theresa's husband, Steve, got a $20,000-a-year raise just a few months after she adopted the principles of a surrendered wife.
- Gina has no idea how much money her husband is making now, but she has a lot more disposable income than she did before she started surrendering.
- Elizabeth's husband won a sales contest, made a huge bonus and got an all-expenses paid trip just a month after she started surrendering. They took the most extravagant trip of their lives.

RELEASE YOUR GRIP

"I had plastic surgery last week. I cut up my credit cards."
— HENNY YOUNGMAN

*E*ven if you're nervous about surrendering the finances, act as if you're confident and follow the instructions below. You can consider it an experiment, if that helps, or, if you need more motivation, think about how exhausted and overwhelmed you are. I know it's not easy, but you *can* do it. Remember to stay focused on all the benefits you'll receive: more free time, more gifts, a greater sense of being cared for, less stress, greater prosperity, and better intimacy.

Here's how you actually go about doing it:

Step 1: Merge Your Money

There can be no intimacy unless there is vulnerability, and one of the ways wives avoid vulnerability (and therefore intimacy) is by controlling the family's cash flow. As an act of your faith in your husband's ability—ability to earn, spend, and manage money wisely—give him all of the money you earn or receive from other sources. Trusting him doesn't mean you will have to go without. It means he will give you cash to buy the things you need, which is just what you would have done yourself anyway.

There's no need to panic. In Step 2 you will discover that you'll enjoy the same standard of living—if not better—as you have grown accustomed to providing for yourself.

I know that if you're a breadwinner, the idea of turning over your entire paycheck sounds particularly loathsome. However, if you've been managing a joint checking account where his money is deposited, then he was doing the very thing you're dreading. If he was willing to do this, why shouldn't you be?

If you've been maintaining separate accounts and separate finances, I strongly suggest pooling your money in a joint checking account that he manages. You've been holding back in a way that may have simply seemed more convenient, but it was also guarded. If what you want is intimacy, you must let down your guard.

Until you are willing to intertwine financially, you will never be able to cross the chasm that keeps you from intertwining emotionally. If these words make your heart race, join the club. You can think of plenty of objections—not to mention the legions of feminists, accountants, and marriage counselors who will say that giving your husband all your money is a terrible idea. Yet, I've never seen it fail to make both husband and wife happier and ultimately more prosperous.

If you're still panicking, keep in mind that you can always go back to the way you're doing things now. Start strong and act as if you have every confidence that your husband will manage the finances as well as (or better than) you did.

Step 2: Make a Spending Plan

When I teach women about making spending plans in my intimacy workshops, someone always incredulously asks me why I would put myself on a budget. The word budget, like the word diet, makes people cringe because it implies an uncomfortable restriction. It brings to mind clipping coupons and suffering through tuna fish lunches.

But a spending plan is different because it allows you to live in the comfortable style to which you have grown accustomed; it is not designed to save money, but rather to predict what you will need each month, on a month-by-month basis.

Only you can determine your needs. Here are some steps to help you devise your spending plan easily and accurately.

1. Predict your expenses based on what you usually spend and remember to be generous to yourself in your plan, especially for the first month.

Get a realistic sense of what you need by keeping track of what you spend for a month. To do this, make a list of your household purchases. For instance, my spending plan includes funds for clothes, makeup, gas for my car, going out with my girlfriends, facials and manicures, books, CDs, gifts, massages, groceries and home furnishings. My spending plan does not include household expenses such as rent or mortgage, utilities, credit card bills, car payments, or other fixed monthly expenses. Nor do I include my car payment, the cleaning lady, student loans, or the cost of going out on a date with my husband. He handles those for us.

My friends who have children cover their children's needs in their spending plans: they account for toys, diapers, clothes, babysitting, entertainment, birthday parties, and all the other things that children need for their health and happiness.

Although my spending plan tends to be consistent, each month I make a new one, so that I don't ever feel hemmed in. For example, if I want to buy a new bedroom set, my spending plan would be unusually large one month. Then, if I'm not going to buy any new furniture the following month, it would drop down to my usual plan again.

2. Tell your husband you want your spending plan money in cash.

He may give you a certain amount weekly, monthly, or on paydays. There are two key benefits to doing this. One, you'll never need to use a credit card, ATM card, or checkbook to pay for anything. Without those so-called "conveniences," it's harder to spend more than you have and easier to figure out what the heck happened on the monthly statement. Two, it's a very powerful feeling to have all that money in your possession.

Having cash gives you autonomy to spend what you want when you want, instead of having to find out if there's money in the checking account first.

3. Don't worry that your husband may not be able to afford your spending plan.

This is not your concern. When you give it to him, it will be up to him to decide if you get all of it. Perhaps you will get more, perhaps you will get less. In either case, you should thank him for the money and make do with it knowing that it is the most he can afford while still keeping the family's other interests in mind. Remember that sometimes you had more and sometimes you had to make do with less when you were managing the money too. As with any gift, receive it graciously. The minute you start complaining, you're no longer being gracious.

4. Once you've developed a generous spending plan for yourself, the most important thing is to live within it.

It is essential for your husband to be able to predict accurately the family expenditures without worrying that you are going to throw him a curve ball in the middle of the month. You also want to maintain your credibility. Sticking to your plan lets him know that you will be taken care of for the month if he gives you the amount you ask for.

Go easy on yourself. Remember, the goal here is not to save money, although if you do (and you very well might), that's great. This is not a good time to quit long-standing habits—such as going to Starbucks in the morning—in order to save money. Don't leave the luxuries out of your spending plan. For now, just indulge yourself, and be sure to let your husband know how grateful you are for that fresh coffee every morning.

5. Revise your spending plan each month.

If you find you really have trouble sticking to your spending plan, you may have underestimated your needs, which is why I reevaluate my plan each month. I repeat: *You don't need to feel hemmed in by your spending plan.*

However, if you continue to have trouble month after month, you may be a compulsive spender. In this case, I highly recommend you contact Debtors Anonymous, which is patterned after Alcoholics Anonymous and provides a spiritual program to help compulsive debtors and spenders learn to make good decisions with money. If you continue to spend or debt compulsively, there is little hope of having true intimacy with your husband. Since DA is a free program, there's no reason to put off contacting them:

Debtors Anonymous
P.O. Box 920888, Needham, MA 02492-0009
phone: 781-453-2743
Web site: www.debtorsanonymous.org

Step 3: Put the Checkbook Down and Leave It There

Proceed with caution on this step, as it's a bit tricky. I've seen some wives who are ostensibly surrendering the finances broach the idea by saying, "You have to take care of the checkbook and give me money for my spending plan."

This is still telling him what to do and does not improve things at all.

When Lynda asked her husband if he wanted to take the checkbook, he said, "No. That's okay." Then she called me to tell me that she couldn't do this part because her husband didn't want to. No surprise. Lynda had not relinquished control. Instead, she had asked for permission to keep control, and gotten it.

Even if you think your husband will be happy to control the money, remember that you are introducing a change to the status quo, and that's always jarring. You will want to approach the conversation with a spirit of humility by telling your husband that you can't manage the finances anymore because you're too stressed out. This is true—you really can't do it and have the renewed intimacy, romance, passion, and emotional connection you want with your husband.

Some women can't bring themselves to say that they can't do the finances anymore, so they announce that they don't *want* to do them, but I don't recommend that. Most husbands hear this as a complaint, along the lines of "I don't want to do the laundry today," rather than as a request for help.

I know you don't like the phrase "I can't." I know women have spent the past thirty-five years affirming that we can do anything, I know that a good therapist might coach you to say "I choose not to" instead of "can't."

However, the problem with eliminating the words "I can't" from your vocabulary is that it makes it very difficult to set limits. Saying "I can't" is a good shorthand for saying, "It's not worth what it would cost me." It's also a great reminder for anyone who's listening (including ourselves) that we're mortal women—not superwomen. Saying "I can't" is more vulnerable and more compelling because you're not just complaining—you're acknowledging your own limits and admitting that you need assistance. Loving husbands always honor a cry for help.

For example, if your child came to you and said, "Mom, I don't want to do my homework," you'd probably respond by saying it's understandable but that she had to do it anyway. On the other hand, if your child said, "Mom, I can't do my homework," you'd probably respond by offering some assistance. See the difference?

GOD DIDN'T PUT YOU IN CHARGE OF THE BILLS

*S*ometimes a woman who is accustomed to paying the bills has come to see it as her job, so when she puts down the checkbook, she feels as if she is not meeting her share of the responsibilities. She will ask me how she can get her husband to take responsibility for her job after all these years. If you feel this way, ask yourself why you believe handling the money is your responsibility. Unless God himself told you that you should do it, you probably just assumed the task years ago. All you have to do now is stop assuming it. You don't have to make your husband take it, you just have to let it go.

I'm not saying it's easy let go, but it is very simple. If you're holding something you can't hold anymore, you just put it down.

A good way to relinquish financial responsibility is to get out the checkbook and say, "I can't pay the bills anymore. I'm just too stressed and overwhelmed." If you want, you can add that you feel he would do a better job with managing the money. That's all you need to say, so once you've said it, STOP TALKING. Then put the checkbook down on a table or counter or some other neutral spot. Don't pick it back up, even if you see it still there several days later.

Do not explain how to balance the checkbook.
Do not tell him which bills need to be paid.
Do not offer any assistance at all unless he specifically asks you for help. He probably won't.

You may be wondering what happened to the part where he picks up the checkbook and happily and dutifully writes the checks without any confusion or confrontation. Don't worry about that. You don't need to control what happens from here at all. Instead, focus on taking care of yourself, which you've already started to do. It's up to him to figure out what to do next, and it may take him a little while to make a decision. You may not get a response like, "Okay, then I'll take it over," but let him take care of it anyway. The only other action you need to take is to give him your spending plan.

It's common for husbands to grumble or object when you have this conversation with them. Remember—don't engage. When Liz tried to relinquish the household finances, Greg expressed his disappointment in her: "I thought we were a team," he complained. "I don't have time to do it because I work so much. It's easier for you to do it."

Just listen to your husband's response. Don't offer to do anything differently. For example, if he says, "Well I certainly don't have time to pay bills," you could just acknowledge that you hear him by saying, "I hear you." This doesn't mean that you're taking it back, just that you're listening. Don't try to fix the problem at this point, because you'll only end up back where you started. Stick to your original declaration—that you just can't do it. No further explanation is necessary.

Fortunately, Liz was able to resist this bait and say nothing. Gregg did take over the checkbook, and later he even took over the books for Liz's business. Some months later, I asked him how he liked handling all the finances for the family.

"I wouldn't have it any other way," he said with a big smile.

Obviously, he was feeling powerful and accomplished at providing so well for his family. Of course, that was partly because Liz had done such a good job with sticking to her spending plan.

REDISCOVERING HIS GENEROUS NATURE

> *"One does not toss out the gold because the bag is dirty."*
> — BUDDHA

*E*ach wife I've suggested these steps to has had a list of objections as long as my arm. Some wives are concerned that managing the household finances will be too much of a burden for a husband who works hard, has health problems, or is not good at math. Whatever your objection, you are really saying that your husband is incapable. You are probably afraid to rely on him.

Have a little faith. Remember, you married this man because you saw that he was smart and capable. Why should you doubt him now? He's still that same dependable guy. Pretend you believe in him, even if you don't feel that way and he will rise to the occasion. I see it happen every time.

Having faith in your husband means that you don't open the mail to see if he paid the bills on time. It means you don't check the balance in the checking account to see what's in there. It means you don't panic when he makes a mistake that costs him money. As long as your needs are met—if there's a roof over your head, gas in your car, food in your refrigerator, clothes in your closet, money in your purse—try not to panic. Give your man the chance to do things for you.

Some wives are concerned that their husbands are stingy and will deny them extras like facials, pedicures or babysitters. Stingy husbands are a common by-product of controlling wives, and in every case I've seen, the stinginess disappears when the wife relinquishes control. You will never know how generous your husband is until you let go of the finances in your home. For a preview of coming attractions, think about whether you found him stingy during your courtship. The man who wooed you is about to return . . . if you'll let him.

MARVEL AT YOUR PERFECT MATCH

Of course surrendering the finances to your husband doesn't mean that he'll never make a mistake. Beth had been surrendering for several months when the phone was disconnected for nonpayment. She was mortified at having to go to a neighbor's to call her husband at work. Instead of berating him or criticizing him for letting it happen, she simply told him the phone was shut off and that she did not like it. Before the day was through, her phone was back on, and Beth had had a chance to talk to other women about how embarrassed and disappointed she felt. When her husband came home from work, she thanked him for paying the bill and resisted the temptation to rage at him. I marveled at her maturity.

Perhaps Beth would have been justified in yelling at her husband that it was unacceptable to have the phone shut off. She could have complained about the inconvenience and embarrassment of looking broke or irresponsible in front of a neighbor. That might have made her feel better in the short run. But shame kills intimacy. Beth kept her eye on the ball: having intimacy with her husband. The choice was hers: She could let the phone disconnection be an inconvenience or a major trauma. Beth chose the former, and although she felt touchy that evening because of that incident, at least there was no fallout with her husband to clean up later.

* * *

The following month, the electricity at my house was disconnected for nonpayment. I thought of Beth and was inspired by her level-headedness. I actually laughed out loud at the irony. Here I was, writing a book telling other women to trust their husbands to pay the bills, and in the process of doing just that, I couldn't even turn on my computer!

The weather happened to be gorgeous, and I wish I could tell you that I took this opportunity to go out in the backyard and enjoy the sun. I wish I could say that we ordered in dinner and lit candles that evening. I wish I could say I had the serenity to let my husband take care of everything.

Unfortunately, I can't tell you that without lying like a rug.

Instead of relaxing, I went into survival mode, located the checkbook, and went to the nearest payment office. I wrote a check even though I had no idea what was in our checking account. The power was back on in a couple of hours, but I had missed an opportunity to trust and relax. When I called Beth to tell her she was not the only one who had had this experience, I realized that I would probably have to live through the whole episode again, just so I could get it right the next time.

Of course I could have focused on how I had trusted John and he had let me down, and I could have decided right then and there that I would take responsibility for the bills again. In that moment I was tempted. But as the poster child for surrendering, I couldn't stop doing what I was telling other women to do. Instead, I was forced to remember that I, too, had made some mistakes when I was handling the money.

I had always paid the utility bills, true, but I'd made some other costly moves. For instance, I started a small business that was a money drain from the time I opened the doors to the day I closed it six months later. I had bought things on credit that we couldn't afford and bounced plenty of checks. I even compulsively bought a small condo that we ended up living in for four dreary years. To me, my actions didn't seem irresponsible because they were *my* mistakes. But if I was going to be fair I couldn't very well point a finger at him without looking at my own shortcomings.

Like water seeking its own level, John and I match: We both had a degree of irresponsibility with money.

It occurred to me then that I couldn't remember a single time that John had criticized or belittled me for my money mistakes. I decided to cut him some slack, particularly since he was doing a job I could no longer handle.

Fortunately, my husband, like most, is a quick learner, and he's never made a mistake paying the utility bills again.

As I've said before, you and your husband match perfectly too. Just because he's a free spender and you tend to be conservative with money doesn't mean it's time to call a lawyer. There are lots of ways to "match." For instance, his overspending may be the shadow side of your tendency to hoard, since neither approach is truly balanced. Perhaps your fear of losing money is the flip side of his ambition to invest aggressively for bigger returns. Maybe you're the one who always has money in the bank, but he's the one who really knows how to have a good time.

One of the gifts of marriage is that as you grow and become more intimate, each of you heals in areas that you might never have expected. You may find your fear of financial insecurity lifts when you know someone responsible and loyal is steering the ship. He may feel his urge to make impulse purchases diminish as he realizes there's nobody telling him what he can and cannot buy. You will both gain wisdom and maturity. Ultimately you will bring out the best in each other as you continue to master this intricate, magical dance.

7

RECEIVE GRACIOUSLY

> *"The art of acceptance is the art of making someone who has just done you a small favor wish that he might have done you a greater one."*
> —Russell Lynes

Make a point of graciously receiving everything your husband offers you, whether it's help with the children, a necklace or a spontaneous shoulder massage. Accept your husband's thoughtfulness good-naturedly and recognize that receiving graciously is the ultimate act of giving up control.

Even if you're not sure you want the gift or think he can't afford it, receive it with open arms and good humor. Be on the lookout for gifts you might not have noticed before.

Make "Receive, receive, receive" your mantra.

*O*nce your husband takes responsibility for the finances, you'll probably notice more gifts are coming your way. You'll want to brush up on your receiving skills so as not to dampen his enthusiasm.

Receiving sounds deceptively easy, but a lot of us have a hard time simply accepting gifts from our husbands. A gift can be either something material that comes in a box (like a new sweater or a necklace), devoting time and effort to unburdening you (like making dinner or washing your car), or a simple sign of his affection and adoration (like a compliment or a back rub).

There are two reasons we sometimes do a poor job of receiving. The first is that we have a hard time believing that we *deserve* the gift, and that it doesn't leave us owing a debt. The second reason is that we often dismiss or reject gifts—especially compliments—in an effort to appear modest.

I struggled for years with feeling undeserving of my husband's gifts. Once when we were dating, the vendors at a street fair got excited when John announced that he would buy me any piece of jewelry I wanted. I thanked him but refused his offer. In my mind, I was calculating what he'd spent on lunch, the boat ride and the movie and thinking I didn't deserve such generosity. At that time, I had little understanding that I was depriving us both of an enjoyable experience because I didn't think I deserved any more special treatment that day.

I had also learned to dismiss compliments as a way of letting everyone know I wasn't arrogant. If someone said I had gorgeous hair, I complained that it was unruly. If they said I was well spoken, I'd argue that I had stuttered and stammered. If they said they were impressed by something I'd done, I'd warn them that it wasn't as hard as it looked, to be sure they knew I wasn't too full of myself. Sometimes I would even react to a compliment with suspicion, in case the kind words were insincere and meant to manipulate me. In reality, I didn't want to be so vulnerable as to accept those compliments.

Receiving gifts of any kind makes you feel vulnerable because you are not controlling the situation. You are not *telling* your husband how he can help you, nor are you *choosing* what you specifically want or *deciding* where and when to go. Rather, receiving—accepting what is put before you—might take you beyond your comfort zone. By its very definition, receiving is a passive act.

This feeling of undeserving becomes evident very quickly in my workshops when I ask everyone to think of an authentic compliment for the woman to her right. Many women struggle to receive the compliment, or feel the urge to make a joke and dismiss it. Often they have a very hard time keeping eye contact, letting the kind words in and saying "thank you."

No One Can Steal Your Independence

Another reason I sometimes rebuffed either a material gift or the gift of help is because on some level, I believed it threatened my independence. For instance, if a coworker paid for my lunch, I might think, "I can take care of myself." I took feminism and twisted it into the belief that I had to do everything myself.

I believe in offering women as many choices as possible: education, a satisfying career, full-time motherhood, marriage, or any combination of these. To me, the goal of feminism is giving more women more choices. I chose to go to college and have a career. I felt so strongly about my identity as a feminist that when I married in my early twenties, I chose not to take my husband's name. I knew my opinion counted, and that I was smart. In fact, I was so independent and capable, I believed I could do anything on my own. I would have been hard-pressed to admit that I needed help from anyone. So, when others generously tried to assist me, I felt that my independence was threatened, but that simply isn't true.

Unfortunately for me, I hadn't learned much about the fine art of receiving.

SMILE AND SAY "THANK YOU!"

> "Welcome anything that comes to you, but do not long for anything else."
> —ANDRÉ GIDE

You deserve to have sweet, beautiful, luxurious things in your life, and your man deserves the pleasure of giving them to you. Start receiving graciously and the gifts will multiply and come with greater enthusiasm almost immediately. If you weren't expecting a gift, if it seems extravagant, or if it's something you don't need, you might be tempted to say, "Oh, I didn't need that." Or, "really, you shouldn't have gone to all that trouble." When you respond with anything but a big, "Thank you," you are rejecting the giver. You are also saying "I don't value my special place in your life." That's a hurtful message. Instead, recognize that receiving a gift graciously is sometimes the greatest gift of all.

Even if the gift is not quite what you had in mind, accept it graciously and appreciate that someone was thinking of you.

UNCOVERING HIDDEN AGENDAS

*R*eceiving graciously means understanding and acknowledging that others feel pleasure when you allow them to give you something. It means that you are open to having presents bestowed on you. Graciousness requires softness and vulnerability—both key ingredients of intimacy. Rejecting a gift, or subtly criticizing it is a hard, cold response that fosters distance—not closeness.

In a practical sense, receiving graciously means that when your husband offers to put the baby to bed, take you to a show, or get you a chair at a party, you smile sweetly and say thank you.

Sounds simple, right? Many women have an agenda that keeps them from being able to accept the things their husbands want to give them. The agendas go something like this:

"If he puts the baby to bed, he will put the pajamas on backwards again."

"He needs to relax after a long day at work, so I'll put the baby to bed."

"We can't afford to go to a show."

"If he picks the movie, I probably won't like it."

"It would be rude to take the only chair, so I'll stand too."

"I don't want to sit next to that awful woman from the PTA, so I won't take the chair he's offering."

These are all valid points, but they interfere with receiving, and therefore with intimacy. When you reject his offers, for whatever reason, you close the door to the pleasurable connection that results from letting him take care of you. You also deny him the pride of providing generously and gallantly. Every time you pass up a gift from your husband, you miss the opportunity to connect with the part of him that wants to please, cherish, and adore you.

RECEIVE, RECEIVE, RECEIVE!

*Y*our opinion does count, and you have every right to express it, but before you do, consider the price. The kids won't die if their nightclothes are on backwards. Criticizing your husband for putting the pajamas on the wrong way, however, will belittle him. Going to the theater probably won't bankrupt the family. Refusing to go out with your husband for the evening or implying that he's being fiscally irresponsible will call his judgment into question and make him less enthusiastic about taking you out in the future. Refusing to sit when he offers you a chair because he's still standing might make you feel more equal, but you'll be denying him the joy of giving and you the pleasure of receiving. Recognize when you do this that you are making a *choice* to sacrifice intimacy to have things your way.

Imagine that at the end of a date instead of standing there ready to receive a kiss, you stood with your arms crossed and glared at your date. It would take a pretty brave or very inconsiderate man to kiss you under those circumstances. If you've ever uttered the words, "Never mind! I'll do it myself!" or even worse, taken action that screamed out that sentiment, you have metaphorically stood there with your fists up when it was time for the goodnight kiss. You have deterred gifts that might have come your way.

When your husband offers to help you, compliment you, or give you something, it's in your best interest to accept graciously and without critical comment. This will not make you appear incapable or undo what women have gained politically and socially, but it will make your marriage more intimate and fulfilling.

I've come to see that receiving gifts graciously requires much more courage and maturity than clinging to a false sense of independence or modesty by rejecting them. Today I have a new mantra that I use to remind myself to take what I'm offered politely. I tell myself, "Receive, receive, receive!"

THE UNEXPECTED GIFT

> *"I praise loudly, I blame softly."*
> —CATHERINE II OF RUSSIA

If you're thinking you would be happy to receive gifts from your husband, if only he would offer them, chances are you've been *overlooking* his gifts. A woman will often dismiss her husband's offerings if they aren't what she has in mind, and therefore miss receiving them entirely. She then feels deprived, as though she's not getting anything at all.

Feelings of deprivation sometimes lead wives to attempt to manipulate their husbands into giving them things. We write notes with lists of chores, set boundaries, or say how hurt we feel if he doesn't get us a birthday present or bring us flowers once in a while. Usually, he responds poorly, dragging his feet and making it clear that he feels burdened. By this time, we are convinced that he is inconsiderate and lazy. Even if he does what we wanted, we are still unhappy because we don't just want him to give us gifts; we want him to *want* to give us gifts.

Take Roxanne and Rich. She complains that he never lifts a finger to do anything for her. It's an ongoing struggle to get him to bathe the kids at night or hand her a diaper, she claims, saying that Rich groans with unwillingness at the smallest request. When I talked to Roxanne at length, however, she mentioned the two bathing suits Rich had gotten her for Mother's Day. Later, she told me he had also offered to put her up at a hotel for the weekend so she could catch up on her sleep. By the time she started complaining about how he had left some spots on the windows when he washed her car, I was on to her. She was completely overlooking her husband's gifts because they weren't the gifts she thought he should be giving her!

In reality, Rich is a generous man who wants to please his wife. When he didn't do what Roxanne asked or told him to do (in other words, didn't respond well to her control), she overlooked all of his gifts and acted as if he never did anything thoughtful. From his point of view, he was doing everything he could to make her happy, and from her point of view he wasn't doing anything that counted. What a mess!

As Roxanne focused on thanking Rich for the gifts she was getting and stopped telling him what to do, she found he seemed much more generous and willing to help her in other ways. Rich was happy to lend a hand with the kids and pamper his wife, as long as he knew she appreciated him.

To better understand how your husband feels when you reject his gifts, imagine yourself preparing a present for a close friend. You've made sure this gift is just what your friend will like. You lovingly wrap the gift and with great anticipation, you present it to your friend. But instead of smiling happily and thanking you, she rolls her eyes. When you ask her what's wrong, she says it just wasn't the kind of gift she wanted, or that you should have gotten her something else altogether. Naturally, you feel rejected. You would certainly think twice before getting a present for this friend again, and you might stop giving her things altogether. An incident like that could seriously dampen your friendship.

If you recognize that you have rebuffed your husband in a similar way—whining when he presents you with a gift or surprises you by doing something extra around the house—don't beat yourself up. You can start receiving from your husband and reverse the damage right now. Most husbands continue to give their wives at least small offerings even after years of being rebuffed. Generally speaking, this is part of your husband's nature—his drive and determination to please his wife will never die completely as long as you're still married. The minute he sees an opportunity to succeed with pleasing you (without being controlled), he'll seize it.

Think hard about things your husband has done for you recently. Write a list of the things he does that you are grateful for to shift your perspective. Just like the optimist who sees the glass half full instead of half empty, you have the option of looking at your husband's gifts instead of his deficits. Don't overlook the things he's giving because you take them for granted—all gifts are precious opportunities to receive.

When I ask women to change their perspective by listing their husband's recent gifts, some wives will insist that their husband really hasn't done anything in the longest time. After some prompting, usually they'll admit that he does make dinner sometimes, or that he mows the lawn without fail, or runs out to the store when the milk is gone. In particular, working to support the family (whether he is sole breadwinner or part of a dual-income family) is a contribution that many women overlook when counting the reasons to be grateful for their husbands. Of course, you may keep the household running or work to earn a living as well. However, just because you are doing your share (or more), doesn't mean you should take for granted the fact that your husband also does his part.

OPENING BOXES WITH BOWS

*"The supreme happiness of life is the conviction
that we are loved."*
—VICTOR HUGO

So what about receiving graciously when your husband gives you something material that you really just don't like? Since this is your lifelong partner and mate we're talking about, you've got to tell him the truth, right? He's going to see how you truly feel by your response anyway, right?

That depends on you. There are two parts to receiving a gift: one is that you receive the gesture of love and thoughtfulness, and the other is that you also accept the giver's choice of gifts. Yes, the material gift is just a symbol of affection, but the two are so intertwined it's hard to accept one and not the other.

I learned the value of the symbolism within a material object when a woman showed me the rings on her fingers. On her right hand, she wore two expensive rings with gorgeous stones, and on her left, only a modest gold band that was pretty banged up. She explained to me that although they could afford better now, the inexpensive band was the ring that meant the most to her because it was the one that represented her beloved husband's desire to marry her all those years ago.

For this woman, the object that represented her husband's love was precious because of what it symbolized, not because it was the most stunning ring in her jewelry box. Think long and hard before you reject a material object because it doesn't meet your usual standards of beauty or style. In reality, you are rejecting much more.

I'm not saying you shouldn't exchange a bathrobe to get the right size, or that you should wear a scarf you hate every day to make sure he thinks you like it. I'm just saying to consider it carefully before you reject it out of hand. This is what he picked out for you because he thought you would like it, and he knows you well, so give it a chance. Of course it's not what you would have picked out yourself. For that, you can go shopping any time.

Often our first reaction to something we wouldn't have bought for ourselves is plain rejection and to criticize (if only to ourselves) that our husband doesn't understand or know us, after all. Corrin told Ray she was very appreciative of the gorgeous handbag he gave her for Christmas, but that it wouldn't hold all of her things. She promptly returned it for another that was more practical. The practical purse was never a source of compliments, she told me, and in retrospect she realized that the sleek one her husband had purchased would have surely made her feel more beautiful. Eventually she told him that she regretted returning the attractive handbag, and that she appreciated his good taste. This opened the door for him to try again without fearing another rejection—a big plus for their intimacy.

Unfortunately, Robin cut her husband Paul absolutely no slack when he gave her a copy of a ring she had admired for their anniversary. He had copied the wrong ring—the one she disliked—and she told him so right then and there. Naturally, the anniversary celebration was not as romantic as Paul had planned. She completely missed the opportunity to receive the love and affection that went into his present. Instead of pride, he probably felt embarrassed and rejected, which crowds out intimacy every time.

Receiving graciously has the pleasant side effect of shifting your focus away from everyday annoyances like finding your husband's socks on the floor. Again. Somehow, noticing gifts makes room for gratitude in space that was once filled with concern for overdue bills, holey underwear and correcting him when he's singing the wrong lyrics to a song. Naturally, you'll feel a greater sense of happiness as a result.

8

FOSTER FRIENDSHIPS WITH WOMEN

> *"When I find myself fading, I close my eyes and realize my friends are my energy."*
> —Anonymous

For an intimate marriage, you need several friends who know you well and whom you can entrust with any secret. Without confidantes, the chances of becoming overly needy or smothering your husband are great.

Take inventory of your closest girlfriends. Do you have at least two or three who will listen and support you as you surrender? If not, you need to make some. Consider being more active at church, parent organizations, volunteer or civic groups or Surrendered Circles so you can meet these new friends. You might want to join a group of people with whom you will find an instant connection through a shared interest.

Conferring with women who are dear to you will make your surrendering journey easier and keep you focused on the rewards.

*Y*our husband isn't the only person you'll need to practice receiving from. Sometimes a friend's listening ear or sympathetic support is an extraordinary gift that may be just as difficult to accept. Still, receiving is an important part of friendship, just as friendships are an important part of surrendering. You'll want to get support and encouragement from your friends as you surrender because you can't very well ask your husband for it. Here's why:

Would you ask your boss if he's noticed that you've been coming to work every day for the past few months? No, because that's a minimum requirement of most jobs. Likewise, don't ask your husband if he's noticed you're not very controlling and critical. Remember that, at a minimum, you owe it to your husband to treat him with dignity and respect.

You'll know you're improving when the tension in your back disappears and you have more energy and warm feelings toward your husband. Take these as signs of encouragement.

But if you're like me, you'll also want your husband to give you a pat on the back. I know it's tempting to say "Don't you like the fact that I didn't tell you to make sure there's no mud on your shoes?" For the same reason that you wouldn't ask for kudos for using a fork instead of your fingers, don't say things like that to your husband. Remember that intimacy and joy in your marriage are the rewards that you're really after.

CONFIDANTES ARE CRITICAL

*"A friend is one who knows you and loves you
just the same."*
— ELBERT HUBBARD

$\mathcal{W}$henever we go through a change, we *do* need support, and
that's why I encourage you to tell other women about your surrendering process and to establish nurturing relationships with them.
First, you will want their encouragement. Second, as with anything
else, having other people who support and share your goals for a
happy marriage will help keep you inspired and motivated. Third,
they can meet some of your needs in a way that your husband simply can't.

Female friends will talk tirelessly and compare notes about
their husbands and their marriage, which your husband can't do
with you. You'll also find women are generally more willing to
delve into feelings than men are and can empathize in ways that
are different from your husband. Your husband will certainly support you too, but not endlessly in every situation. That's why you
need someone who will listen and sympathize but who isn't im-
pacted directly by what you're saying, or who doesn't mind kick-
ing things around for a while. That doesn't mean you can bash
your husband endlessly, but you do have my permission to let off
steam—as long as in the end you remind yourself that you married
a guy you respect. Pick someone to talk to who will gently hold
you to this standard.

You will also need women as a source of emotional sustenance
because no one person—not even your husband—can meet all of

your needs for human interaction. Without a few friends to talk to, you'll feel clingy and needy around your husband. He may pull away to avoid being smothered, and probably feel disappointed that he can't meet your expectations.

To give you a sense of this dynamic, imagine yourself in one of the following situations:

- You've just lost a pregnancy and you're completely devastated. You look to your husband for support, but he is just as crushed. He becomes frustrated and short-tempered with you, particularly because he feels powerless to fix the situation and make you happy.
- You're angry with your husband for coming home from work late again, and you're tempted to tell him how fed up you are. You need perspective on the situation, and you certainly can't get it from him.
- You're mad at your mom again, and naturally you need to talk about it. Your husband says you should tell her what's upsetting you, which is probably good advice, but you're still feeling upset. You want to keep talking about it, but he doesn't.

You might need to have the same conversation about your mother with three friends *and* your husband just to get through your feelings. That's not uncommon for a woman, but it's a rare man who can take the place of three girlfriends who are good listeners. You'd be asking an awful lot if he was the only one you talked to about your sadness or anger.

How can you tell when you've exceeded your husband's ability to support or willingness to talk about something? You'll know because you'll feel frustrated when you bring up that topic. He'll take a sudden interest in the newspaper, try to change the subject, start tinkering with something, or tune you out. Worse, he may tell you to get over it, or that it's no big deal. You may be tempted to scream at him to listen to you, but it's hard to create intimacy and garner support by screaming. I've tried it. It never worked.

Other women have had frustrating or puzzling experiences with their husbands, just as you have, and can offer validation about what you're going through. Yes, men seem strange at times, and yes they have different needs and values that are difficult to understand. Just knowing that someone else has felt the same way can be amazing comfort.

Another benefit of hooking up with other wives is that just being with a group of women makes you feel womanly. As a child, my mother lived in a multifamily home in Long Island with her grandparents, aunt, uncle, and cousins. I was always fascinated to hear her describe how much she loved to gather in the kitchen with only the women and girls to talk. A phone call to a friend or female relative can give you a whopping dose of the same feminine spirit.

Think about how rejuvenated you've felt after a baby or wedding shower where only women are in attendance. Chances are you've felt great because you've simply basked in being a woman and in sharing perspectives and experiences unique to women: You've honored your feminine spirit.

An important part of staying intimate with your husband is to remember who you are and what it means to be a woman. You won't get many reminders at work, so look for them elsewhere.

9

RESIST BITING
THE BAIT

*"I argue very well. Ask any of my remaining friends. I can
win an argument on any topic, against any opponent. People
know this, and steer clear of me at parties. Often, as a sign
of their great respect, they don't even invite me."*
—DAVE BARRY

Your husband may chafe at the changes surrendering
brings to your marriage at first, and try to get you to go
back to the old ways by using bait.

Do your best to avoid giving him advice, even if he
asks for it. He may squirm or complain, but he'll always
figure things out eventually. If your husband asks you
what he should do, deflect the question by encouraging
him to do whatever he thinks he should do. Each time
you resist the temptation to "bite the bait," congratulate
yourself on your progress.

$\mathcal{S}$urrendering will disrupt your husband's routines just as it does yours, and he may resist the changes, either consciously or unconsciously.

For instance, if he's used to hearing you tell him where to turn when he's driving, and you've decided to stop giving him directions, he'll probably ask you which exit to take on the freeway. If you've been telling him which ties to wear for years and one day you don't, he may wonder out loud which one he should wear. He will unconsciously make every attempt to follow the usual script. His chief weapon will be Really Big Bait.

Really Big Bait is anything that makes you want to engage in a familiar conversation or argument. It's asking a question to get a certain answer. It's saying, "Knock, knock" with the expectation that your partner will respond with, "Who's there?"

Let's say he's now taking care of the bills. The very next thing you know, he may come bursting into the room with an important declaration such as "I don't know how we're going to pay the mortgage this month!"

Make no mistake about it: This announcement is an engraved invitation for you to jump up and do the same old dance that you've been doing together for years. He's trying to get you to engage. He's trying to get you to take over again because now there's a problem and he's not accustomed to fixing it because that used to be your job.

You might be tempted to say, "Let me take a look at the numbers," or "How much are we short by?" or "Take some money out of the savings then." If you offer any of those answers, you are in effect saying, "I wasn't really serious about giving up the checkbook.

Forget the whole thing and I'll take it over again. That way I won't have to be nervous and you won't have to be uncomfortable."

Instead, say, "I'm sure glad you're taking care of that for us." Remind him that he's in control of that now, and that you're grateful. Letting him make his own decisions, without punishing him for making the "wrong" decision later, keeps you from taking on unnecessary worries, and restores his sense of power and masculinity—but only if you can resist taking them on again.

HE'D RATHER HAVE YOUR BLESSINGS THAN YOUR OPINION

"The greater part of our happiness or misery depends on our dispositions, and not on our circumstances. We carry the seeds of the one or the other about with us in our minds wherever we go."

— MARTHA WASHINGTON

Your husband might ask your opinion about whether he should go back to school, take a river rafting trip or how to handle a situation at work. In each of those instances, he needs to do what he thinks is best, even if you're afraid you'll never see him during the semester, or that he doesn't swim all that well or that he'll lose his job.

Of course we all like to be asked our opinion, but you need to resist giving it here for two reasons:

1. Your husband already knows what to do.

By telling him what you think, you risk contradicting him. No matter how much he wants to know what you think, he wants to know that you bless what he thinks *more*. If your ideas don't match, there will be friction, guilt, resentment, or all of those.

If he asks which job you think he should take, what he's really saying is "Do you think I'll make the right decision?" If he asks you what you think about his plan to buy a certain stock, the question is not whether he's making a good decision, but whether you *trust* him to make that decision. I know it sounds like he's asking for your input when he says "What do you think?" What he's really saying is "What do you think of my ability to handle this situation?"

2. As long as you worry about his decisions for him, he knows he doesn't have to take the consequences into consideration.

When you let go of his worries (or at least act like you're letting go) he has to pick them up again. He'll feel ownership of his life because that's what happens when you stop controlling him. You'll preserve your energy for yourself instead of feeling depleted from worrying about something that's his responsibility.

You can avoid taking the bait by saying, "Whatever you think," and trusting that your husband will make the right decision.

LITTLE BAIT IS TEMPTING TOO

> *"There can be no defense like elaborate courtesy."*
> — E. V. LUCAS

*O*f course, not all bait is really big. Some bait is small, but just as tempting. Your husband might ask you for a phone number you don't know off the top of your head. Resist the temptation to look it up in the phone book for him. Resist the temptation to tell him there is such a thing as a phone book. Say, "I don't know" when you don't. Use this phrase, or a rhetorical response such as "That's a good question!" when he throws out bait like this:

When is the car registration due?
Which frying pan should I use?
What should I order for breakfast?
Where's the mayonnaise?
Where should I park?
How much should I leave for a tip?

When you don't give these questions specific answers, you may feel a loss of control. The fear underneath that control might rear its ugly head. Perhaps you will worry that the tip was inadequate, or that your Teflon pan will get scratched, or that your husband's cholesterol will get too high if he eats bacon and eggs.

Telling your husband that you'll go along with whatever he thinks is a powerful way to deflect bait and remind him that you're not interested in doing any of the old dances. You are also forcing him to meet new challenges, whether it's keeping track of the automobile paperwork or learning about omelet pans through trial and error. He can handle it.

Resisting bait will make you feel vulnerable because you'll suddenly lose control of things you're used to controlling. However, trusting his judgment has its own rewards: He will feel more self-assured and masculine, for one thing. His increased sense of competence and your relief about not doing everything are both good ingredients for intimacy.

THE LURE OF STRONG, SILENT BAIT

> *"The best cure for anger is delay."*
> — SENECA

*Y*our husband might also try to engage you without saying a word. He might let bills stack up in a box without even opening them and ignore calls on the answering machine from creditors. He might quit his job and not try to get another one. He might let the baby cry for much longer than makes you comfortable. You can jump in and save the day, but as soon as you do, he no longer has to worry about creditors or jobs or babies because, thankfully, you're worrying about all of that for him. Once again, he sees that you don't really expect him to take care of things. Now you're right back where you started—doing everything yourself.

In the case of silent bait, even mentioning the situation is taking a big bite. There's no need to make any announcements or have any discussions with your husband about how you're going to stop responding to his silent bait. In fact, such a conversation would be counterproductive and insulting, because you'd really be accusing him of dropping the ball and letting him know that you were over-seeing the whole situation just in case he failed. Instead, just ad-dress silent bait in kind—silently. Reassure yourself that he's taking care of the situation, and you don't have to worry. This is part of his process. The sooner you let go of it, the sooner he'll grab the ball and run with it.

WHEN TO GIVE YOUR OPINION

The only times you wouldn't want to refer your husband back to his own thinking is if he's asking you to choose something based on your desires, such as where you want to go to dinner, what color car you like, or which apartment you'd rather live in. In these instances, go ahead and say what you prefer. If, however, he asks you which computer *he* should buy, how to dress the baby, or whether to refinance the mortgage, use the phrase "Whatever you think."

If your husband is asking for validation about something he's done, don't confuse that with bait. Give him the reassurance he re-quests. For instance, if he asks "What do you think of the way I trimmed the bushes?" or "What do you think of the way I waxed the car?" always be positive. Say, "The bushes look a lot neater" or "That really makes the car look shiny." He's not asking for your advice here, just reinforcement, so give it to him. Everybody needs that.

Your Mantra: Don't Engage!

"You will find as you look back upon your life that the moments when you have truly lived are the moments when you have done things in the spirit of love."
— Henry Drummond

*Y*ou may find yourself exasperated when your husband invites you to advise him over and over again. You may resist the bait the first eight times, only to give in the ninth time he asks the same question. Fortunately, as with practicing any of the principles of a surrendered wife, you don't have to be perfect. Soon your husband will learn not to ask you about things that he can figure out for himself. Continue to exercise your "surrendering muscles," and you too will learn not to engage.

Now that you recognize bait and know when he's inviting you to engage, you will be able to resist taking it and falling back into those old, controlling habits. You may get irritated when you spot bait. You might think, "If he would just stop baiting me, I would stop telling him what to do!"

The bad news is, it doesn't seem to work that way. You have to change your habits first. The good news is that as you stop responding to his bait, he will stop using it. After all, if he finds it doesn't do him any good, he'll eventually stop wasting his time. He'll do his own thinking, and take initiative, just like you've always wished he would.

10

AVOID SETTING UP
A NEGATIVE EXPECTATION

> *"Treat people as if they were what they ought to be, and you help them to become what they are capable of being."*
> —GOETHE

Consider your words carefully before you speak to make sure you are not setting up a negative expectation for your husband. Remember that how you see him influences how he sees himself. Treat him as though he is punctual, patient, tidy or successful and he will rise to meet your expectations.

The more you act like things are going to turn out well, the more often they do. You manifest what you focus on, so when your husband's actions (or lack thereof) make you nervous, act carefree, as if you believe the outcome will be good.

*B*y constantly controlling my husband, I often unwittingly set up negative expectations for him. I subtly but clearly let him know that I expected him to screw up, drop the ball, let me down, and make a mess. I call these spouse-fulfilling prophecies. Not surprisingly, he lived up to my expectations. Unfortunately, my behavior is not that uncommon. Many wives do the same thing.

Interestingly, men take a great deal of their self-perception from their wives. If a wife tells her husband he is always late, bad with money, or a lousy dresser, he tends to believe it on some level. He might reason that because she is the person who knows him best in the world, she's probably right.

My friend Nathan told me a story that illustrates this point. While he was making smoothies in the blender, his wife recalled a single incident from a few years ago. She turned to her friend and said, "Watch out! He always breaks the wooden spoon in the blender and puts splinters in the smoothies." Sure enough, Nathan did get the spoon too close to the blade and make splinter smoothies. He even had a sense that she "made" him do it. Of course she didn't, but he felt that his mistake was already a *fait accompli*.

If you tell him he's not good with money, or doesn't know how to take care of children properly, or can't change careers at his age, you are helping to reinforce that belief for him.

I criticized and corrected John because I saw him as I was *afraid* he was, not as he really is. And it was not until I stopped giving my doubts a voice that my opinion changed dramatically. He seems so much stronger, more confident and accomplished now. Is that because I let go of my negative perspective, or because he started to see a better picture when he looked in his wife-mirror?

I may never know, but I do know this: This change is very real to both of us.

IF YOU TELL HIM HE'S GOING TO SCREW UP, HE PROBABLY WILL

"If you keep on saying things are going to be bad, you have a good chance of being a prophet."

—ISAAC BASHEVIS SINGER

*H*ere are the kinds of things we frequently say that have negative expectations attached to them:

"Don't you think we should slow down a little?" (Expectation: You're going to crash the car.)

"You have to rinse the dishes before you put them in the dishwasher." (Expectation: You're not going to do a good job.)

"Why don't you just call a plumber?" (Expectation: You can't fix it yourself)

"If I were you, I wouldn't put up with that from my boss for one minute!" (Expectation: You're not going to stand up for yourself.)

All your husband hears is, "I don't expect you to do very well in this situation." In each of these statements is the strong suggestion that we expect our husbands to screw up. All that's left is for him to do is prove us right.

Advertisers recognize the power of suggestion and use it to their advantage every day, as in "How about an ice-cold refreshing Coca-Cola?" If you were a billboard that your husband saw on his way to work, would you read, "You forgot to go to the post office again, didn't you?" or "You're as reliable as ever—thanks for going to the post office!"?

Expressing negative expectations to your husband is not only potentially harmful, it's also a huge waste of breath. If you take an honest look at your relationship, you will realize that you have never really accomplished anything with negative comments. Chances are he doesn't spend any more time with the kids, go to the doctor any more frequently, or eat any better than he did before you started pointing out his shortcomings. People don't tend to improve because you've revealed their obnoxious behavior to them. At best, they make a half-hearted attempt; at worst, they rebel and do the opposite. After all, when you behave like the negative mom, he's likely to show up as a rebel without a cause.

Most people tend to respond to positive reinforcement, trust, and respect.

ACT AS IF YOU HAVE FAITH, ESPECIALLY WHEN YOU DON'T

"Confidence is contagious. So is lack of confidence."
—MICHAEL O'BRIEN

What if I just don't believe it?" some women ask me. "What if I'm really afraid that he's screwing up?"

When we're in the thick of our marital loneliness, the future does seem bleak, and you may not be truly optimistic about it. But you do have to *act* like you have faith that your marriage will improve. Therefore, one of the keys to success in surrendering is to pretend you have faith—or, as the old expression goes, to "fake it 'till you make it."

You may feel like an actress at times, putting on a cool pose when you're terrified and thanking him for things that don't seem to be enough. But I promise, there's no better time to do an acting job worthy of an Oscar nomination than when you're surrendering.

The more you act like you respect, trust and appreciate him, the more you'll start to believe that he deserves that treatment, and the less you'll worry about trying to run his life. When you have faith in your husband, even when you're stretching it, you will bring out his very best efforts and awaken his tenderness. You'll begin to remember why you wanted to marry this man in the first place, and he'll go to new lengths to please and pamper you.

Acting in faith is the flip side of setting up negative expectations. He will not want to disappoint you when he sees that you trust him to succeed in his work, feed the children something nutritious, and invest the savings wisely. Acting in faith means that while you might have the fleeting thought, on a bad day, that you should call a divorce lawyer, you don't dwell there. If you have faith that you can have a happy, satisfying marriage, you don't think about divorce lawyers for long.

If You Can't Say Something Nice . . .

> *"Become a possibilitarian. No matter how dark things seem*
> *to be or actually are, raise your sights, and see possibilities—*
> *always see them, for they're always there."*
> —NORMAN VINCENT PEALE

*A*cting in faith and being gracious doesn't mean that you lie or betray yourself. It does mean finding the goodness in the situation even when the bad seems ten times as prominent.

My husband was going to make a presentation for a job interview where he knew his qualifications were weak, but his enthusiasm was high. Although he'd had days to prepare, he started writing the presentation just a few hours before his interview. I agreed to watch him rehearse and was horrified when my articulate husband started stuttering and contradicting himself. When he looked to me to for feedback, I pretended that I had every faith that he would do a terrific job by saying, "You've done this sort of thing so many times, John. Of course you'll be great." I didn't say, "Gee that was a terrific presentation!" or "I can see you've really prepared for this," because those comments wouldn't have been true.

As soon as he left for the interview, I called a friend and told her that I was afraid my husband might have a disastrous presentation. It turned out, however, that my faith, and not my fear, was correct. He came home all smiles. The presentation had gone so well, they offered him the position on the spot.

Again, you're not necessarily going to *feel* this faith. You're going to have to muster it. In *The King and I*, the English schoolteacher is nervous about being in a new country with new students. She admits that the way she summons her courage when she's afraid is by whistling a happy tune. In the song, she talks about how she not only fools everyone around her into thinking she's confident, she even tricks herself into feeling it!

She makes a decision not to succumb to her fear. Rather than staying in her homeland where she felt safe, she got on a ship bound for Siam. Rather than hiding under the bed once she got there, she showed up to teach the king's children. She acted in faith that she would not just survive, but enjoy these experiences—and so she did.

You, too, can make the decision that something else—an intimate marriage—is more important than your fear that you'll be embarrassed or let down by your husband.

Ambrose Redmoon wrote, "Courage is not the absence of fear, but rather the decision that something else is more important than fear." When you're surrendering and looking for intimacy, acting in faith is more important than giving in to your fears.

11

STOP READING
HIS MIND

"It's better to ask some of the questions than to have all the answers."
— JAMES THURBER

Avoid trying to guess what your husband is thinking. Give him space to express himself. Remember that you can't accurately read his mind or draw conclusions before you hear what he has to say.

If you still think you know what your husband will say or do before he does it, write down what you anticipate your husband will say or do if you tell him, for example, you want to go out to the movies. Then, tell him you want to go to the movies and compare what you wrote to what he actually says or does.

One day, my friend, Theresa, said she knew her husband was angry with her because he scowled when she walked into the room.

"Did he say why he was mad at you?" I asked.

"He didn't have to," she told me. "I know it's because he thinks I'm spending too much on therapy."

"How do you know?" I probed.

"I just know how he is," she countered.

I identified with Theresa's perception that she could read her husband's mind. I had often presumed to "know" what my husband was thinking based on his grunting, slamming, disinterest, or other nonverbal signals. When John grimaced at me without saying anything, I assumed he was angry at something *I* had done or said.

When he failed to change a burnt-out lightbulb for weeks, I assumed he was inconsiderate and oblivious. When he watched television shows I didn't care for, I assumed he had poor taste. I even thought he was doing (or not doing) those things to irritate me.

As a surrendered wife, however, I learned that many of my assumptions and interpretations had been based on my fear. Fear that I was not meeting John's expectations or living up to my responsibilities in some way, and that he was "retaliating" in a nonverbal way.

My psychic abilities were not as accurate as I had thought. When I took the time to listen to my husband's words, rather than presuming I knew how he felt, I was often pleasantly surprised.

Once I looked up from reading a magazine just in time to see him slamming the newspaper down in what seemed like anger.

Somewhat startled by this, I asked him, in an agitated tone, what in the world was the matter! Just then he picked up the dead fly he had just killed.

IF IT'S NOT THE LOOK OF LOVE, DON'T TRY TO FIGURE OUT WHAT IT IS

> *"Each of us has his own little private conviction of rightness and almost by definition, the Utopian condition of which we all dream is that in which all people finally see the error of their ways and agree with us."*
> — S. I. HAYAKAWA

*I*nstead of regarding an ambiguous face as a call to battle, I made a decision to do nothing until he spoke to me directly. If my husband had a bone to pick, I reasoned that he would tell me in a straightforward way. Only small children need someone to help figure out whether they're angry, frustrated, hungry, or tired by the look on their face. If John wants me to address something, he tells me plainly. Otherwise, I assume and trust that he's working everything out himself, and I go along my merry way. This works beautifully.

When I made a conscious effort to stop drawing my own conclusions, I learned that the scowl I thought was for me was actually intended for my sister-in-law. The burnt-out lightbulb in the socket reflected that his priorities are different from mine. The tasteless television shows were popular not just with my husband, but with many other men I know and respect who seem to find entertainment in places I never could.

The Important Role of Duct Tape in a Happy Marriage

As with other principles of surrender, I wasn't perfect when it came to shutting down my mind-reading habit. Initially, I just rechanneled it. I had a habit of "interpreting" my husband for other people. He would say something, and I would pipe up and tell them what he meant. I actually thought I was being helpful, but in reality I was interrupting him, before he could get a sentence out. When we went for marriage counseling, I even tried to tell the therapist what he was saying! Obviously, I don't recommend this. Now, I just get out the duct tape—double-strength, if necessary.

I also had the habit of reading his mind even if he was speaking it. For instance, when my husband said that he liked his new job, I didn't believe him. I was noticing that he seemed drained and listless every night when he came home. I jumped to the conclusion that he was not being truthful. Later I told John that when a friend had asked me how he liked his new job, I had responded by saying, "He *says* he likes it." I might just as well have said, "I doubt and disrespect him, and don't put any stake in what he says." Why would I want to give anyone that impression? How unattractive, insulting, and inhibiting for intimacy.

Today, I try always to take John for his word, even if what he says isn't entirely convincing. Just as I "fake it till I make it" sometimes, he may be doing the same, and I certainly don't want to contradict him. As it turns out, John *didn't* much like that job and ended up leaving after a short time. Still, I respect that he tried to maintain a positive attitude while going there every day. My harping about how I could see he was miserable was unsupportive and therefore made it harder for him to keep his chin up during that difficult time.

Unless your husband tells you something directly, don't assume it. Even if you're a bona fide clairvoyant, reading your husband's mind does little to enhance your relationship because nobody likes to be second-guessed. A scowl doesn't always have to be about you. As much as we might like to *think* we know what's going on in his heart and mind, we don't. Imagining that we do is a waste of energy that could be better spent on our own self-care.

WHEN HE'S IN A FUNK, LEAVE HIM ALONE

"Fear is that little darkroom where negatives are developed."
— MICHAEL PRITCHARD

*W*hen you feel the need for reassurance, look to your girl-friends to remind you of the ways he's been thoughtful and sweet recently. Pull out your wedding pictures and think about how good you felt that day. Make your own gratitude list of things he's done that show he loves you, but don't ask him to expound on his affection for you when he's distant or grouchy. Instead, let him be.

I recommend doing whatever you need to do to avoid getting entangled in whatever situation is putting him in a bad mood. Get out of the house, visit a friend, watch television, or read a book. Distract yourself with self-care. His mood will pass eventually. The only constructive thing to do is to wait it out without inviting him to talk about the issue with you, since you're not his mom or his therapist.

Of course if he volunteers to talk about what's going on with him, then you'll want to be a good listener as you reflect your trust and respect. There's no need to avoid this conversation; just don't try to start it for him.

Remember: Let him work out his own problems and don't put yourself in harm's way by looking for tenderness when his is on hiatus.

STAY IN THE MOMENT

"Do not dwell in the past, do not dream of the future, concentrate the mind on the present moment."
— BUDDHA

I have noticed that many of us pride ourselves in "knowing" how our husbands will react to a given situation. The logic goes something like this:

- I already know what he's going to say before I talk to him.
- I don't like what he would have said if I had talked to him.
- I am disappointed and angry with my husband because he didn't say the right thing when I *didn't* talk to him.

On the other hand, maybe you don't mind the answer you assume your husband will give, but you're completely *bored* with the fact that you always know what he's going to say and therefore never have to ask him. That one goes like this:

- I already know what he's going to say before I talk to him.
- This "same old, same old" thing sure is getting dull. I wish my husband would say something different once in a while.

- I am now bored with my husband because he would have said the same thing he always says *if* I had talked to him.

In the examples above, you are now irritated with your husband even though he has not even spoken to you. Anticipating your husband's reaction is the same as reading his mind. Just as you can't know what he's *thinking*, neither can you know what he's going to *do*.

Every second you spend thinking about what he's probably going to do or say is another second that you miss interacting and connecting with him in the present. Seconds turn into minutes, which turn into hours and days. Some women spend their entire marriage anticipating instead of connecting, which means they never get the chance to be intimate. A good rule of thumb is to avoid dwelling on thoughts that start with the word "if" because they're not about the present. You cannot anticipate and be intimate at the same time.

Jessica got a sizable bonus at work and was lamenting about how her husband would spend it on stocks instead of the vacation she'd been longing for. I reminded her that she didn't know for sure what he would do with the money, and to just enjoy the possibilities for the moment, and that she could always tell him what she wanted.

She resisted this at first, but then admitted that she certainly wasn't finding any enjoyment in complaining about his choices before he'd even made them. Instead, she focused on how proud she felt that her family would have something extra from her bonus—even though she didn't know what it would be. She soon admitted that celebrating and enjoying the satisfaction she felt at providing an unexpected gift sure beat thinking about how she would feel *if* he did something she didn't like. In fact, thinking about being disappointed is as bad as actually being disappointed.

Anticipating is a second cousin to setting up negative expectations. If you are anticipating hostility or stinginess based on his response before you surrendered, you're setting up a negative expectation. To cultivate intimacy with your husband, listen to him instead of preparing an argument for what you imagine he is going to say. Focus on really hearing and understanding his words instead of interpreting his tone and expression.

Only once you've heard him is it fair to say that you know what he thinks.

12

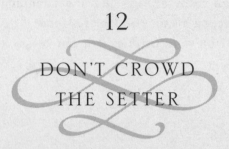

DON'T CROWD
THE SETTER

> *"Few things can help an individual more than to place responsibility on him, and to let him know that you trust him."*
> —BOOKER T. WASHINGTON

Give your husband space. If he is supposed to take care of something, let him take care of it. Even if you think he will have trouble (or can't do it), mind your own business.

Remember that your husband can meet whatever challenges arise and learn his own lessons as necessary. Trying to fix everything cramps his space, undermines his abilities and emasculates him.

I love to play volleyball, and I love to be the setter—the player who receives the ball from a passer and puts it up high enough for the hitter to slam it over the net. As a general rule, the setter always gets the second ball unless she calls for help. This rule keeps people from crashing into each other or letting the ball hit the ground unnecessarily.

Inexperienced players sometimes worry that the setter won't be able to get to the ball in time. They try to "help" by standing under the ball so that they can set it if necessary. This is called crowding the setter. I hate when that happens because when I try to set the ball, there's someone standing in my way. I might even drop the ball because I can't get past my teammate. Often the inexperienced player will turn around and say, "Why didn't you call for help? I could have gotten it!"

Indeed!

If the rookie had stayed out of my way, I would have given her a beautiful set and the satisfaction of pounding the ball into the other team. Instead, she was too busy crowding the setter—worrying that I wasn't going to do my job and then blaming me when I couldn't get past her.

Did I mention I *hate* when that happens?

ONE LESS WORRY FOR YOU

"When a man points a finger at someone else, he should remember that four of his fingers are pointing at himself."
—LOUIS NIZER

So what does volleyball have to do with surrendering to your husband? Just as crowders worry that a setter won't do her job, you may worry that your husband won't do what he's supposed to—and then get in his way. If you hover around him under the pretense of being ready to help, you're really making his job much harder. You're also dragging your team down, and you're blaming the wrong person for your troubles.

Crowding the setter is just another form of control. When you try to get your husband to go somewhere on time, suggest that he call the plumber, or remind him to pay something before there's a late fee, you're crowding him.

Just as I don't feel much team spirit for the volleyball player who gets in my way, don't expect much intimacy from a man when you've invaded his space.

HE DOESN'T NEED BACKUP

Better a hundred enemies outside the house than one inside.
—ARABIAN PROVERB

*E*ven if you're not saying anything to your husband, you can still crowd him by putting energy into what he's doing. Checking on the pile of bills to see what he's paid—even when he's not around—is a form of crowding the setter. Listening to a phone conversation he's having with a client, being on alert in case he asks you where to turn, and wincing because he shouldn't have said something are all examples of crowding the setter.

You don't even have to say something to crowd your husband, because he can read you like a book. He's so familiar with your expressions and body language that he can sense when your energy is all over what he's doing. He can feel you breathing down his neck. If you've just been in his stuff, he'll sense your presence lingering in the way you've left the chair at his desk, or unconsciously straightened the papers in his "to-do" pile. Therefore you need to keep your energy to yourself so he has the space to take care of things as he deems appropriate. He needs space to be independent. That's true for anybody, and most especially true for a man.

Although Ken and Kelly had a standing agreement that he would take the kids to school in the morning, Kelly often got up early and got dressed, "just in case." Ken did indeed run late sometimes, or complain just before car pool time that the morning was too busy for him to transport the children. He would ask Kelly to take the kids for him, so she fell into the habit of always being on call. One day it occurred to her that he was shirking his responsi-

151

bility simply because he knew that she was there for backup. In this case, she ended up crowding him *and* cramping her own style, waiting around for the ball to drop.

Finally, Kelly decided to stop "crowding the setter" by staying in bed later and trusting that everything would work out fine. Amazingly, when Ken realized there was no backup, he stopped running into trouble in the mornings and consistently took their children to school.

As best you can, stay out of your husband's space and remind yourself that you don't have to anticipate anything going wrong. Remembering that he's got everything under control will help curb your own urge to control.

Not only that, you'll be giving the setter enough space to put the volleyball up in the air so the hitter can slam it over the net.

Did I mention I *love* when that happens?

13

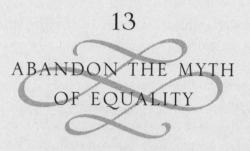

ABANDON THE MYTH OF EQUALITY

> *Nature is unfair? So much the better, inequality is the only bearable thing. The monotony of equality can only lead us to boredom.*
>
> —FRANCIS PICABIA

Instead of throwing out traditional gender roles, try them on again. There may be some value in them that you would like to reclaim. They can help you feel protected and feminine, and therefore more intimate.

Practice "changing your hat" when you leave work. A surrendered wife can be a force to be reckoned with at work and a soft, gentle woman in marriage, as long as she surrenders when she comes home.

*A*s a modern woman, I expected that my husband and I would divide the work in our marriage equally according to our strengths. I believed we would come to the relationship as individuals, rather than limiting ourselves to outdated gender stereotypes. I presumed that we would share the housework evenly and decide together how to invest our savings. Perhaps he would stay home with the children while I ran a big corporation. Everything would be negotiated rationally, so that together we would find the best possible life. We would have a true partnership.

We never realized my egalitarian vision. In fact, we never even came close. Still I kept thinking if we just tried a little harder, we could do it. Gender just didn't matter! I knew that because everything I'd grown up with, from Marlo Thomas's *Free to Be . . . You and Me* to Betty Friedan's *The Feminine Mystique* said this was so. It never occurred to me that the model I was using was impossible to live by.

The trouble started when I noticed that my strengths seemed more practical than John's. His fun-loving good nature didn't seem useful when it came to the serious business of paying a mortgage and maintaining the cars. I loved to hear him play the guitar and sing to me, but that didn't help with getting dinner on the table every night. His contentment with life started to seem like laziness when he resisted doing home-improvement projects.

I found fault with everything John did because he didn't do it the way that made sense to me as a woman. When he handled the finances, I was appalled because he didn't methodically plan them out. I wanted him to maintain the house by fixing every little thing as soon as it started to crumble, and by adding bells and whistles all the time. John's style, of course, was different and masculine.

He was more concerned with security and function in our home than he was with beauty. He thought nothing of paying bills as they came due instead of planning ahead. Many times he tried to do things my way as well as he possibly could, which of course wasn't very well since he was going against his own nature.

I was trying to make John into a Laura, but obviously he could never be a good me. Instead of taking the initiative to do things *his* way, he tried to keep the peace. To do this he kept a low profile around the house. I complained he wasn't doing his share.

There were other problems, too. Each time I tried to work in a high-powered corporate setting the long, structured hours made me miserable. John worked from home and I envied the flexible schedule that allowed him time to nap in the middle of the afternoon or stay up late on a weeknight. When I earned more money than he did, I was resentful that the pressure to maintain our standard of living rested on *my* shoulders. I lamented that John's standards of tidiness were not as high as mine.

When I examined why I was so miserable, I found some deeply buried expectations. It wasn't that I wanted John to bring the same things to our marriage that my father had brought to my parents' union. Rather, I wanted John to bring the exact same things to our marriage that *I* was bringing to it—everything from money to a solid sense of order, social planning, decorating . . . and everything else that women typically find important.

Since we were both 50 percent responsible for everything, and I liked my way of doing things better than his, I took responsibility for 99 percent of everything from maintaining the home to planning vacations. Although we were talking, the back and forth wasn't equal. When John did or thought about things out loud, I let him know with my body language, voice, or facial expression the minute I thought he had hit a wrong note.

In my head I rested comfortably in the notion that our marriage was an equal partnership, but truth is, I was in charge. I assure you, it was *not* equality.

ONE SKIRT AND ONE PAIR OF PANTS

"The woman is the fiber of the nation. She is the producer of life. A nation is only as good as its women."
— MUHAMMAD ALI

One of the reasons the division of labor failed when I was first married is because I tried to pretend that there was no gender difference. Of course, that didn't make it so, nor did it make us happy.

We feminists have struggled with acknowledging—and even tried to deny—that as women, we still want to be protected, pampered, spoiled, adored, pursued, and treasured. Sure we can shatter glass ceilings and take care of ourselves, but then what? Truth be told, I still wanted to hear that I have pretty hair and I longed to be held and taken care of when the working day was done.

Having a man's protection puts us at ease. Receiving his gifts makes us feel special. Knowing he desires us makes us feel attractive and sexy. And, for equality's sake, when he pleases us and wins our admiration, he feels proud, sexy, and strong.

That's how men and women are made, and these natural gender roles don't make us weaker or less capable, nor do they make men brutish or domineering. We don't need a man to hold the door open for us, but we love how feminine we feel when he does.

As it turns out, the new division of labor John and I have is based partially on the strengths each of us brings *because of our re-*

spective genders. For instance, while I was stressed out and resentful about making most of the money at a corporate job, John is happy and proud to be the primary breadwinner. While I'm neurotic about finding the perfect living room furniture and window treatments, John couldn't care less what our house looks like—as long as I'm happy. Instead of showing him couches and saying "Do you like that one?" I now acknowledge that couches are much more important to me than they are to him and say, "I like this one." While managing the finances made me pull my hair out, John has a more relaxed approach that lets him make levelheaded decisions. I pretty much run the social calendar and invite people for dinner parties, which John enjoys but rarely initiates. We accept each other's different interests and priorities.

I was amazed to find out how many of the traditional gender roles worked better for us than the so-called "equality" of sharing everything, but there are things about traditional roles that don't fit for us. For instance, I would hate to give up my work and income to be a stay-at-home wife. I don't like to clean, so we have a housecleaner. He does the dishes and mails out the greeting cards for the holidays.

You could argue that with our current arrangements we have divided the work according to our strengths, rather than our genders. In some ways you would be right. But understanding the unique characteristics of our genders, rather than pretending that we were identical, helped me get there.

DISLODGING ROUND PEGS FROM SQUARE HOLES

We commonly confuse closeness with sameness and view intimacy as the merging of two separate "I's" into one worldview.
— HARRIET LERNER

 o, how can I advocate that women surrender to their husbands and still identify myself as a feminist?

I believe that feminism addresses what I want at work, but says little about what to do in my marriage. In the workplace, I would never settle for anything less than equal pay, equal opportunity, and having a voice equal to my male counterparts. But at home, those qualities contribute nothing to the romantic, intimate relationship I want. With John, I am softer and more flexible, a feminine spirit who delights in being attended to.

People sometimes ask me why the roles in a marriage can't be reversed. Why can't the husband defer to his wife and tell her what he wants? Perhaps they can be reversed; however, it did not work for me, and it wasn't working for the women I know who adopted the principles of surrendering in their marriage. John Gray has some ideas about why that is.

In *Men Are from Mars, Women Are from Venus* Gray put forth the best-selling message that men and women are indeed different: psychologically, emotionally, aspirationally. I was relieved because for years, so many of us had tried so hard to say that despite the obvious physical differences, men and women were alike. He says women are Venusians and men are Martians. Said another way, women are round pegs, and men are square pegs. Naturally then, women are more comfortable in round holes and men are more comfortable in square holes. When a woman embraces the feminine role in her marriage and the man embraces the masculine role, everyone is more comfortable.

True, a square peg can go into a round hole, and vice versa, but we all know how uncomfortable that is.

Eastern philosophy describes the same concept using the words yin and yang. Yin is the spirit of the female and yang is the spirit of the male. These two concepts are represented by shapes that fit together exactly and form a perfect circle.

This Is the Best Time in History to Have an Intimate Marriage

"Communication is a continual balancing act, juggling the conflicting needs for intimacy and independence."
— DEBORAH TANNEN

I am not implying that the 1950s when "men were men and women were women" was a panacea. Whether a woman stays home maintaining a "traditional" role has little to do with how intimate her marriage is. Perhaps my prefeminist grandmothers would have had an easier time admitting they liked to be taken care of than I do, but otherwise, I suspect they knew little more about being intimate with their husbands than I did when I first got married. The behaviors that lead to intimacy are rooted in virtue, self-understanding, and maturity, rather than social conditioning or a bygone era.

I don't know of a period in history that we could "return to" to find better emotional and spiritual connection in marriages than we can have now.

If anything, the remarkable peace and prosperity we've enjoyed in recent history puts us in a better position to foster intimacy in our marriages than ever before. Our mothers and grandmothers—who were preoccupied with immigrating to new countries, finding enough to eat during the Great Depression, sending their husbands and sons to war, and tending to lots of children—had little time to contemplate the behaviors that foster romance and passion.

We have more privilege now than ever before, and with this comes the opportunity and luxury to cultivate tender marriages, harmonious families, and our own integrity.

In some ways, feminism has also given us an even greater prospect for intimacy because we now have the ability to *choose* vulnerability and trust, rather than being forced into it economically or socially. Knowing that we can live on our own and then deciding not to is far more meaningful than depending on a man because we have a gaggle of kids to take care of and no means to earn a living. If we stay in our marriages and continue to trust and respect our men now—with the freedoms to own property, have bank accounts, and get divorced—it's only because we want to. Thank you Susan B. Anthony, Margaret Sanger, and Elizabeth Cady Stanton for working to win us these freedoms.

Since I've been very public in describing my relationship with my husband, the people I work with professionally—my agent, my editor, and media contacts—know that I wear a feminine hat when I'm with John. I'm pleased to report that they treat me with no less respect knowing that I prefer to be treasured, pampered, protected, and adored when work is over. My experience with being treated well in the workplace supports my theory that the two arenas—work and home—are quite different and distinctly separate.

Obviously, a woman can take care of and protect herself and her family. Of course, a man likes to be taken care of at times. I'm not suggesting these gender-specific roles are the only way to live, but trying to deny how my gender effects my nature brought out the worst in me and put a huge strain on my marriage.

14

SET LIMITS BY SAYING "I CAN'T"

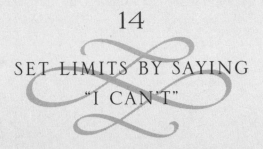

> *"Knowledge of the self is the mother of all knowledge. So it is incumbent on me to know my self, to know it completely, to know its minutiae, its characteristics, its subtleties, and its very atoms."*
> —KAHLIL GIBRAN

If your husband (or anyone else) asks you to do something that will make you resentful, overtired, lose your dignity, or interfere with your self-care, practice saying "I can't."

Until you recognize your own limits and start to honor them, peace and harmony in your marriage will elude you. Also, you'll never get to see how much your husband wants to help you until you admit that you need help.

$\mathcal{B}$efore I surrendered, I did everything myself for one very simple reason: I wanted everything done *my* way. I liked the glasses in the cupboards put in upside down, and the dishes set to soak in the right-hand side of the sink. I preferred to take the freeway to our favorite restaurant because it was quicker than driving the surface streets. My voice graced our answering machine so I was sure it would give everyone who called just the "right" impression of our marriage and home.

I didn't give John the chance to do anything—from picking out a new computer to making an appointment with our accountant for taxes—because I knew he wouldn't do things the way *I* wanted them done. Every time he tried to help, I rejected him for one reason or another. Eventually, he stopped offering to do things.

After a while, I concluded that he was lazy and inconsiderate. I resented him for leaving everything up to me. At the time, I didn't realize the obvious: I was setting both of us up for unhappiness.

THE HIGH COST OF DOING IT ALL

*"I cannot say whether things will get better if we change;
what I can say is they must change if they are to get better."*
—G. C. LICHTENBERG

The truth is, I didn't really want help back then—at least not as much as I wanted to dictate. But keeping authority over every decision came at a very high cost. After so much rejection, John pulled away. I traded the intimacy I could have had to get my way all the time. Today, I'm not willing to pay such a high price.

The message I was sending was that I had everything under control, which I did—*my* control. It hadn't occurred to me that I was actually obsessive rather than efficient, and insulting rather than endearing. I didn't act like I wanted help, but that was only half of me. The other half desperately wanted to collapse in an exhausted heap and know that the world wouldn't come to an end in my absence. I was betraying the part of me that was lonely and forlorn by putting on an aura of impenetrability.

Even when my husband thanked me for something I'd done, there was no amount of gratitude that could erase my feelings of resentment about having to do everything. When he complimented my efforts, it simply wasn't enough for me. I heard his nice words as a manipulation to make me do even more.

It's difficult to escape this cycle, unless we recognize that it's happening, because the pattern is self-reinforcing. Here's how it looks:

1. The wife gets burnt out, and tries to get her husband to help by barking orders or "choring" him.

2. The husband then jumps up to complete the tasks, but not out of kindness—he's trying to avoid further conflict. With this source of motivation, he is not likely to do any more than the absolute *minimum* required so that he can get out of the way fast. He might also just dig in his heels and *not* do the chore to prove that nobody can tell him what to do.

3. The wife, dissatisfied with his effort (or lack thereof), be-grudgingly decides that it's just easier to do it herself. She feels more alone than ever, and criticizes her husband for being lazy, childish, etc.

4. The husband is reminded that the woman who knows him best in the world finds him entirely inadequate. He returns to his distant, protective semicoma, and both are worse off for the exchange.

SAY THE MAGIC WORD (HINT: IT'S NOT PLEASE)

*"All of us at certain moments of our lives need to take advice
and to receive help from other people."*
—ALEXIS CARRELL

*I*f you're feeling exhausted and overwhelmed all the time, I have a revolutionary prescription for you: practice saying these words: "I can't."

If going around saying you can't do things sounds like a nutty suggestion to you, you are certainly not alone. The typical control-ling wife is used to bucking up, persevering, and toughing it out regardless of the cost. She is capable and smart, and doesn't appear to need help, nor is she accustomed to admitting any kind of weakness. However, when she does invite her husband to help, he sees an opportunity to be the hero, to be chivalrous and win her enduring adoration and gratitude. His drive to feel heroic and proud is going to be much more powerful than the contrary motivation he will feel about doing something to get you off of his back. He'll take greater care, go to greater lengths and be more thoughtful when his goal is to earn your affection rather than avoiding your wrath.

A surrendered wife is quick to ask for help, and she does it in a way that makes the man feel necessary and needed. This is entirely different from barking orders. For example:

CONTROLLING: Why don't you carry our toddler into the house?

SURRENDERED: I can't carry him. I need the help of a big, strong man.

CONTROLLING: You try paying the bills around here. It's not easy!

SURRENDERED: Paying the bills is making me nuts. I can't do it anymore.

CONTROLLING: You better get on the phone and get a handyman to come over.

SURRENDERED: There's something wrong with the water heater, and I don't know what to do. What do you think?

You could argue that you *can* handle these situations and you *do* know what to do. But before you go down that old dirt road, consider the cost. You *can* do everything if you're willing to be frazzled and edgy all the time. If you want to be intimate with your husband and have more free time and relaxation, you really *can't* do it all. From this moment forward, pay special attention to anything that makes you cranky and start admitting that you just can't do it. Sadly, you've probably been doing things for years that have cost you too much.

Phillipa felt pressured to get the furniture moved out of their old apartment over the weekend so a tenant could move in on Monday as planned. She picked up the phone book on Saturday and started calling moving companies which would have to charge double because of the last-minute notice. In the meantime, her husband was asking her how long she was going to be on the phone and telling her that he was hungry. Indignant at his lack of concern for getting moved and his utter lack of appreciation for her efforts, she explained the urgency of the situation to him—*again*. Phillipa complained that he was acting like a small child when she wished he would help her. Of course, her husband saw no need to help her because she had already taken over.

Now she was feeling stress from both the original problem of trying to find movers and from wondering how she could get her husband to grow up. She made some more calls, albeit resentfully, and had no luck finding movers to come that day.

Phillipa was still fretting about it the next morning, and complained to her husband that she just didn't know what else to do. Anxious to solve the dilemma, her husband called a few friends and asked them to come and help him move furniture for a few hours. By dinner, the entire apartment was empty and ready for the new tenant on Monday morning.

Phillipa hadn't needed to do a thing. She then realized that it wasn't necessarily up to her to take over this task in the first place. Her husband was well aware of how badly they needed to move the furniture, and even knew how he would do it. If Phillipa felt resentful about single-handedly taking on a shared responsibility, she had the option of just leaving it alone and letting her husband handle it.

When Gary asked his wife, Shawna, to watch the neighbor's

kids along with theirs so he and his friend could spend the morning playing golf, she simply told him, "I can't." He was surprised by her reaction, and said "Why not?" She replied honestly by saying that she didn't want the responsibility of watching extra kids when she had errands mapped out for the day.

Gary found another solution to his problem. He rounded up a teenager who lived on the street and agreed to pay her for a few hours of baby-sitting.

Andrea's husband was preparing to leave on a business trip when he turned to her and said that he didn't have time to pay the bills before he left and asked if she could do it for him.

Andrea wisely said the magic words, "I can't." While her instinct was to be helpful, she also felt a surge of pride pulse through her when she stayed true to her commitment to herself not to take on the burden of handling the finances instead of rescuing him. Sure enough, he found time to come home from work and pay the bills before he left town, and Andrea avoided a resentment that could have cost her the intimacy she had come to value so much.

LOOK FOR THE HERO IN YOUR HUSBAND

*Y*ou may wonder if this approach will actually work with your husband. Remember that men generally want to help their wives and give them gifts. They like to be the hero, if we will give them the chance.

Consider the results of a *Candid Camera* gag. The setup was a woman walking around with one shoe off and limping badly, barely able to walk. She approached some unsuspecting men and asked them to help her get where she was going. Implicit in her approach was the phrase "I can't walk."

One of the men she approached—a stranger—actually picked her up and carried her to her destination. The *Candid Camera* crew tried it again with another man, and again the man picked her up and carried her. By the end of the episode fifteen men had carried the woman to her destination. These men were every size, age, shape, and race, and all of them had the same response: Rescue a woman who needs help.

Is your husband really so different than the men captured by the *Candid Camera?* You will never know until you admit that you need help.

RESIST TAKING ON THE WORLD

"If a woman can only succeed by emulating men, I think it is a great loss and not a success. The aim is not only for a woman to succeed, but to keep her womanhood and let her womanhood influence society."
— SUZANNE BROGGER

One last hint: You'll also want to resist expending your energy unnecessarily in conflicts that show up *outside* of your home.

If the landlord, principal, store clerk or the city council is causing you grief, do your best not to engage in a battle. Instead, guard and protect your energy for yourself and your family. Let your husband know that you need help in dealing with these annoying people.

When Stephanie felt that her son's teacher was impatient with him, she marched down to the school to speak to the principal. In no time she felt overwhelmed by her and the teacher and school psychologist who also came to the meeting. Everyone seemed condescending and uncaring.

As Stephanie left the school with the problem still unresolved, she remembered that her husband, Joe, was ready and willing to defend their son and that all she had to do was ask for help. Stephanie and Joe went to the next conference together and he did most of the talking. Stephanie noticed that his physical stature and crossed arms commanded respect. She was relieved that her complaints were finally being heard. Ultimately, the teacher treated their child with more courtesy, and everyone was happy.

But there's more: Joe felt proud of how he had protected both his wife and child and that made him feel successful, which made him feel strong. In turn, he felt more willing to show his love for his family. Intimacy replaced aggravation, and now Stephanie even had the energy to enjoy it.

Your husband will probably also feel proud to protect you, if you'll let him. You'll love all the fringe benefits—harmony, safety, rest, and intimacy—that go along with acknowledging your limits by saying "I can't."

If your husband addresses a conflict for you, he'll probably do a great job because generally men don't bring as much emotion to their interpersonal situations as women do. Instead of putting on armor, rely on him to go to battle when it's appropriate, then stand behind him for protection and to lend the support that your presence provides.

On the other hand, your husband may let the whole thing slide because—again—he's not going to feel as much emotion about it as you do. He may deem it unimportant and walk away. When he does, just let it go. Adopt your "So what?" attitude.

It's not your job to put the world right by making sure that the school principal is punished for not doing a good job or that the phone company improves its customer service. Fixing those problems isn't nearly as important as feeling calm and unburdened so that you can put your energy into creating an intimate marriage.

Nurture yourself and your children instead of taking on the entire world. To put the world right, first put your own self right by focusing on how you feel and what you need. Remember that you can't fix the phone company or the principal, but you can heal yourself.

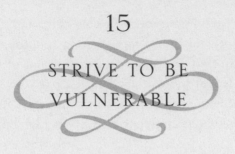

15

STRIVE TO BE VULNERABLE

"Do you want me to tell you something really subversive? Love is everything it's cracked up to be. That's why people are so cynical about it. It really is worth fighting for, being brave for, risking everything for. And the trouble is, if you don't risk everything, you risk even more.

— ERICA JONG

Strive to be vulnerable with your husband by baring your most tender feelings and admitting when you're hurt rather than covering it with anger. When you feel the fear of being rejected or abandoned welling up, find your courage by reminding yourself that you are safe with your husband.

Keep in mind that you can be intimate with your husband only to the degree that you are willing to show him your soft underbelly, because vulnerability is the part of us that connects with other human beings.

Vulnerability is not the same as weakness—it actually takes much more strength and courage to risk emotionally than it does to stay defended.

*S*urrendering requires that you purposely make yourself vulnerable. You must take some risks to have the kind of marriage you crave.

Being vulnerable with my husband means letting my tears come instead of masking my hurt with anger. It means that even when I feel attacked, I put my fists down and let him see that I am fragile. It means holding steady even when I realize I could be rejected or abandoned when I'm the least prepared for it.

But why would I do any of that? Why take those risks at all?

Because I can enjoy intimacy with my husband *only* to the degree that I can be vulnerable with him. Thus, a critical part of surrendering is striving to be vulnerable with your husband.

When you are unguarded, you reveal the part of you that naturally connects to another human being. You remind him of your humanity—and his—and you inspire his masculine instinct to protect and support you. (Remember the *Candid Camera* gag?)

When you let down your guard, the truth comes out in an endearing way, and you feel the incomparable pleasure and joy of being loved just as you are, not for who you think you should be. Intimacy and closeness spring from the relief of admitting you're not at all perfect, and finding out that you're still lovable. Intimacy thrives when you relax in your own skin—without having to be vigilant—because you know you're safe.

OVERRIDING YOUR SURVIVAL INSTINCTS

*"Intimacy requires courage because risk is inescapable.
We cannot know at the outset how the relationship
will affect us."*
— ROLLO MAY

$\mathcal{S}$urrendering to your husband may make you feel more vulnerable than ever before. Even your own survival instincts will scream at you that being vulnerable in your marriage is insanity. You risk heartbreak and disappointment when you reveal your true desires and feelings without masking them with anger or control. The reward for taking that risk, however, is that your husband will have the opportunity to respond with tenderness instead of defensiveness. When your iron curtain comes down, he will feel safe to reveal himself, too. Instead of breaking your heart, he will hold it tenderly.

Some people may tell you that surrendering is appalling because it is "so sexist and antifeminist." They will claim that the mind-set I am suggesting is a throwback to the 1950s, and that you will be giving up the equality and independence women have gained.

Their underlying message is don't let yourself be too vulnerable.

I understand this because I once thought of vulnerability as something to avoid. I thought that people who were vulnerable were weak, which was a terribly unattractive quality for an able-bodied and strong-minded woman to present to the world. Today, however, I strive to be vulnerable in my marriage, and I consider my ability to go to that tender place one of my best qualities. I no longer think of my vulnerability as repulsive; instead I recognize that it's attractive.

The most attractive part about it is the glow that comes from having that magical feeling of knowing that you are passionately and tenderly loved and that you love back completely. When you're intimate, you know traits about each other that you never show to the rest of the world, and you find each other even more attractive and wonderful because of those qualities. You feel certain that he will never use what he knows against you, because you shared it with utter trust and confidence that he is honor-bound to hold in safe hands.

Sharing that kind of intimacy naturally clears the way for affection and love because it removes the barriers of defense. Your passion was there all the time, but you couldn't feel it through the distance between you and your mate. The same urgent impulse to intertwine that you felt when you first met is still there, and when the conditions are right, you feel it all over again.

This primal and spiritual state perpetuates a healthy sex life, the willingness to hang in through hard times, a spark of excitement in what would otherwise be an ordinary day, and that enduring look of affection you sometimes see from couples who have been together for a very long time.

Tell Him You Miss Him

In the old days I used to tell my husband to stop watching so much TV. I would implore him to cut his late hours at work. I told him I needed help with the yard. Of course what I really wanted was for him to pay more attention to me. Needless to say at this point, my strategy was worse than useless.

I now have a more vulnerable and more effective approach, which I'll explain.

Let's suppose you want more attention—more romance—in your marriage. Let's suppose further that your husband is gone a lot because he works too much or plays golf frequently. You might feel that if he would just work or golf a little less and stay home a little more, he would have more time to for you. In your mind, whatever is taking all his time is preventing you from having long conversations, candlelight dinners and bubble baths for two. You might begin to resent whatever he does while he's away because, in your mind, you are in competition with that activity for his time and attention.

Megan felt this way about her marriage. Her husband, Steve, was in a high-tech business and frequently worked late. She often told him she was sick of his working so much and that she needed help around the house. Of course, this didn't keep him home more.

Steve probably felt defensive and unappreciated too. I've heard men say things like: "Doesn't she realize that the reason I work so hard is for her?" Megan's requests probably sounded like pressure to her husband who was trying to balance the needs of his job with those of his family.

After surrendering, Megan learned that beneath her obvious feelings of anger was a more vulnerable feeling: loneliness. She missed her husband when he was gone a lot. Asking him to do things or "choring" him was her way of getting him to stay home. Instead of drawing him to her, her constant nagging was repelling him.

The turning point for Megan and Steve came when she found the courage to tell him what had been true all along: that she missed him!

As you can imagine, this approach had an impact. Steve didn't say much, but he smiled and looked at her appreciatively. To her surprise, Steve managed to leave work earlier twice that week.

By letting him know she longed for his presence and his company, Megan was complimenting him where she used to harangue him. She made him feel important and needed on an emotional level, rather than just a utilitarian one.

The next time you find yourself wishing your husband wouldn't read, watch TV, work, golf, or tinker so much, tell him you miss him. Say it as often as you feel it, even if you are self-conscious hearing the words come out of your mouth.

No Matter What You Miss Your Message Is the Same

Some women object to telling their husbands they miss them because they say that's not how they feel. "I'm just overwhelmed taking care of the kids by myself all the time," they tell me. The truth is these women *do* miss something about their husbands. Whether you miss his help disciplining the kids, his masculine presence, or your lover's touch is immaterial. There's only one message to convey: You miss him!

I know that it will take courage to deliver this message, but remember your husband loves your tender side. Think of how much dignity you'll feel when you don't hear yourself screeching and complaining like your mother on her worst day. Imagine how much energy you'll save and harmony you'll enjoy when you pass up the temptation to complain in favor of revealing your deepest feelings. If you crave romance, I assure you this is a worthwhile risk.

16

ADMIT IT WHEN YOU'RE HURT

> *"The married are those who have taken the terrible risk of intimacy and, having taken it, know life without intimacy to be impossible."*
> —CAROLYN HEILBRUN

All husbands say hurtful things to their wives from time to time. It's tempting to retaliate by jabbing him back. Unfortunately, that sets you up for a full-blown fight where you both walk away wounded.

If you can avoid "hitting" him back, you'll steer clear of further injury on both sides and raise the level of kindness in the marriage. When your husband says something hurtful to you, respond by saying "ouch" and then leave the room if you can. When you don't punish him for his comment by hurting him back, you preserve your dignity, and the potential for intimacy and peace reaches heavenly heights.

*Y*our husband says things that hurt your feelings sometimes. I know this because that's what happens at my house, too. If you're like me, your first instinct is to say something harsh right back. That almost always sparks a fight around here. While I hate to admit it, there's a part of me that actually likes to have a good fight with John. Maybe I'm drawn to the drama and excitement, or the emotional release.

Despite my perverse attraction to brawls, I'm not willing to pay the high price of the silence and coldness anymore. I try to stay out of them completely. Miraculously, we rarely tangle now. For me, the key to avoiding conflict has been resisting the temptation to strike back when I feel stung. It's the same instinct I had in third grade to kick somebody who pulled my hair. It's not easy to give up retaliation, but it can be done. I never learned how to do it until I surrendered.

One effective way to avoid retaliating is to say "ouch!" when your husband verbally punches you and then leave the room so that you aren't tempted to follow up with that hurtful comment that's on the tip of your tongue. That's it. Just say "ouch," then walk away. You don't need to explain why his words hurt your feelings or demand an apology or say anything else.

He'll get it.

When I suggest this, some women complain that it sounds goofy to them. What I hear hidden behind this complaint is that it feels too vulnerable. Saying "ouch" is as good as telling your husband he made a direct hit to your jugular. Of course, our instinct is to conceal our weak spots so that we appear invincible—if he never knows we're hurt, we reason, then it's just like not being hurt at all, right?

Wrong.

Your husband already knows where to find your Achilles' heel. Saying "ouch" is not giving him any new information. While he may seem like the enemy in the heat of battle, he's not. You're both on the same team. Showing him a soft underbelly is a good way to remind him of this.

LET UGLY COMMENTS STAND ALONE

"Silence is one of the hardest arguments to refute."
— JOSH BILLINGS

*W*hen you don't scream at him or complain about what he's said, your husband will hear only his own voice of reproach. He'll also feel sheepish about injuring you when you don't respond in kind.

For instance, suppose your husband says "You've never been very good with money" and instead of saying, "Well you don't make very much either, do you!" you simply say, "ouch!" With the old system, once you bit back, he could justify his behavior by reasoning that you're no picnic to live with. If you refrain from making a nasty comment, there's no need for him to rationalize his words or to defend himself from your emasculating comment. You've left a quiet space where he must face the stark ugliness of just having injured the woman he loves most in the world.

INSTANT KARMA'S GONNA GET YOU

> *"When we were children, we used to think that when we were grown-up we would no longer be vulnerable. But to grow up is to accept vulnerability."*
> —MADELEINE L'ENGLE

*W*hen you throw out a hurtful comment, chances are high that your husband will respond in kind so that you get hurt too. So every time you say something injurious—even if he started it—you are actually giving him cause to strike back. Not that you're responsible for his actions—you're not, but the surest way to avoid getting a black eye is to stay out of the fight in the first place. As soon as you engage in a battle with your mate, instant karma's gonna get you.

Saying "ouch" instead means you get to keep your dignity. This magic word also restores peace in a hurry. Using it is a way to be true to yourself and honor your feelings without persecuting anyone else. This approach requires maturity and fosters intimacy. Eventually, laying down your arms will be second nature as the sense of safety and harmony increases in your home.

Best of all, you will be teaching your husband the finer points of treating you tenderly. Chances are, he'll learn them quickly and be more careful in the future.

17

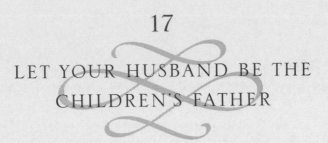

LET YOUR HUSBAND BE THE CHILDREN'S FATHER

> Children are natural mimics who act like their parents
> despite every effort to teach them good manners.
> —ANONYMOUS

Your husband won't always be a perfect father, but
having your respect and support for his decisions will help
prevent unnecessary power struggles and preserve family
harmony. Your children have a mother and a father for a
reason, so try not to interfere with your husband's
contribution to their upbringing.

If your husband is short-tempered with the children,
check to see if you've been respectful. The quickest way to
restore harmony for the whole family is to make
apologies where you have been disrespectful.

Make a list of the things your husband does differently
from you as a parent. How are his methods better? (We
already know you think your methods are better, but just
go along with this for now.)

*I*f the idea of taking care of their two-year-old daughter and the neighbors' two boys overwhelmed Carolyn's husband, Kevin, he didn't show it.

During Kevin's watch, one of the boys got diarrhea that ran down the legs of his overalls. Kevin quickly took the boy out in the backyard to hose him off in the warm July sun. The boy seemed to enjoy this, and it took care of the mess. Still, Carolyn and the boy's mother were surprised that a grown man wouldn't think to use the bathtub to clean him.

Jean was just as surprised when she came home, late in the morning one Saturday, to find her two sons still in their pajamas watching cartoons. Although their father had been supervising them, an empty box of cookies was the only evidence that they had eaten breakfast that morning.

Claire was always shocked to see her daughters flying high in the air after their father tossed them up there. He always caught them—granted, but she would never have done such a thing.

Mothers are sometimes nervous when fathers do things differently. But part of surrendering means accepting that just because your husband has a different style doesn't mean that he's a bad dad. Carolyn's husband did clean the boy. Cookies for breakfast may not be the most nutritious way to start the day, but they're probably not much worse than sugary cereal, and Jean's boys didn't go hungry. Claire's girls were entertained and safe in their dad's strong hands. The fathers got the job done, they just did it differently.

EVEN THE BEST MOTHER IS NOT A GOOD FATHER

"Ward, could you talk to the Beaver?"
—JUNE CLEAVER

Only a woman knows how to be a good mother. Only a man knows how to be an effective father. Therefore, any time a woman tries to direct how her husband fathers, she is in unfamiliar territory, and that's no place to exercise control. By the same token, since I don't have children, I have no idea how to be a parent. I would be way out of line telling you how to do it, particularly if you've got more on-the-job training than me. Instead, I will just report on what I have witnessed in the relationships when I have had the privilege of watching the family dynamics before and after the wife begins to surrender.

For instance, before Candace started surrendering to her husband, Joel, she worried that he spent too little time with the boys and let them watch too much TV. She also wanted Joel to be gentler with her precious babies. She let him know she disapproved of their constant wrestling and roughhousing, which Joel seemed to encourage.

After she began to surrender, however, she quickly realized that she was hurting her family when she interfered in her husband's relationships with his own children. Joel was grumpy when he felt restricted and criticized as a parent; and the two boys were missing out on having happy, peaceful parents. Besides, whether we like it, wrestling is a chief activity for the healthy, developing man-child in our species.

SOME THINGS ONLY A DAD CAN DO

Fatherhood is pretending the present you love the most is soap-on-a-rope.

— BILL COSBY

So what does it look like to surrender to a man in the parenting realm? Don't complain because he dressed your daughter in a pink shirt with red skirt, or your son in the pants he outgrew last summer. The same rules apply here that apply to surrendering in general: Don't criticize, don't offer advice, don't correct or instruct. This will have a positive effect on the entire family.

In addition, make a point of referring your children to your husband for permission or help, particularly if you're the parent who spends the majority of the time with the kids. For instance, if the family is at a store and your child approaches you and asks if he can have something, you could refer him to dad by saying, "Whatever your father thinks." If dad says no, the answer is no. Contradicting your husband's decision undermines his authority, and boy, do men *hate* that.

When Tina's girls saw her treating their father with more respect, they began to follow suit. Several weeks after she had begun surrendering, her thirteen-year-old daughter Brittany was flipping through a magazine and came across a quiz called "Is Your Husband a Grown-Up?" When Brittany started asking Tina the questions in regards to Gregg's grown-up-ness, Tina stopped her and told her that of course daddy was a grown-up. She added that the article was inappropriate and disrespectful.

Later that night, Brittany thanked her dad at the dinner table for giving her money to spend at the book fair. Tina knew they had turned a corner when she noticed the girls asking their father for what they needed more frequently. As Tina changed from treating Gregg as if he weren't good for much to having regard for his decisions and input, the children naturally saw him as more authoritative. In the past, they had perceived Tina as the authority figure and bombarded her with questions. Now, she was relieved from the pressure of feeling like the only parent because there were clearly two parents in charge.

Prior to surrendering, both Tina and Candace were concerned that their husbands neglected the children. In reality, their husbands were withdrawn from the family out of self-preservation, knowing that whenever they were with the children they would be attacked or criticized. This is not to say that the mother is responsible if the father has a poor relationship with his children. She is not. However, a man who feels respected and accomplished is far more likely to show up as a good father than one who feels criticized and defeated.

Just like the old television show *Father Knows Best,* your husband does know better than you do when it comes to being the dad. Dads are the only parents who can teach sons how to be men, and teach daughters how they should expect to be treated by a man. Moms are the only parents who can teach girls how to be women, and impart a healthy knowledge of women to their sons. Dads discipline differently than moms do, and moms nurture differently from dads. The two roles are complimentary. Ideally, children get both influences as they grow. Sometimes dads seem too harsh, gruff, or insensitive. Even so, it's in your best interest, as well as your children's, to leave fathering to him. When you find yourself criticizing what he does, ask yourself what it is you are afraid will happen to the children. He may not protect them perfectly, but then again, neither can you.

During a Surrendered Circle, one woman complained that she

didn't feel safe leaving her children with their father because when she came home, they sometimes had scratches or bruises. Other women nodded emphatically when she said this, and everyone turned to me to find out what I had to say about that. I had no idea what to say, as this sounded pretty serious. Fortunately, my wise friend Anita, mother of three and step-mother of two quietly said, "I notice that my children get scratches and bruises when they're with me, too." Anita helped me realize that we want to hold our husband to impossible standards at times, like expecting our children to be perfectly safe in his care. No matter how responsible or attentive the father, he would always fall short of this expectation.

If you are struggling to have compassion for your husband's mistakes when it comes to the kids, think of all the things you've done as a parent that you wish you hadn't. Now imagine he had criticized you each time you made those mistakes.

CHILDREN RESPECT PEOPLE YOU RESPECT

If your mind isn't open, keep your mouth shut too.
— SUE GRAFTON

Kids of all ages take their cues about who has authority in the home from their parents. If mom doesn't respect dad, then why should they? This is especially true of teenagers. For instance, I've noticed that older children will sometimes look for validation from their mother that dad is mistreating them. If your child wants to complain about his dad, it's okay to listen, but it's essential to maintain proper respect for your life partner during the conversation. Maryanne's daughter, a college freshman, was upset that she didn't get more attention from her father, particularly since her dad was so enamored with his new grandchild. Maryanne and her daughter had spent years commiserating about this until Maryanne started surrendering.

The next time the daughter wanted to complain, her mother listened patiently, but instead of cosigning her grievances, she gently reminded her of all the things she was getting from her dad— like full tuition at college, excellent advice about summer job opportunities, and his help maintaining her car. She reminded her that his concern for her education, choices, and car, was a manifestation of his concern for the safety and happiness of his beloved daughter. Once again, staying in gratitude and modeling it for our children is a powerful way to keep a healthy perspective on how very fortunate we really are.

What Daddy Says, Goes

If you continue to reinforce that what daddy says goes, he'll have less to prove.

Kelly had a hard time referring her children to her husband, Jerry, when they took their son to an amusement park. In the past, she had taken him without Jerry and had made a ritual of buying the boy a lollipop when they were there. In an effort to start relinquishing some control, she asked Jerry if he thought their son should have a lollipop, and he said no. Kelly was sure he was being too harsh and was terribly unhappy with this response. She bit her tongue anyway in an effort to respect his decision. That day, their son had no lollipop. Fortunately, the boy was little and easily distracted by the other wonders at the amusement park, so he didn't have a fit.

Hearing this story, I felt that Jerry had been completely unreasonable. Why couldn't he just buy the candy and uphold the ritual, which is so important to kids? It was such a small thing. Still, I was impressed that Kelly managed to bite her tongue and go along with what he thought that day. She relinquished her authority in favor of respecting her children's father. Not having a lollipop hardly constituted a hardship for their son, who found plenty of other things to delight in at the park. Imagine what the price would have been had she not respected him in this "small" matter? Jerry would have felt undermined (read: emasculated) and angry. He might have inappropriately directed anger at somebody smaller than him, later.

The next time they went to the amusement park, Kelly had been respecting Jerry for some time, and everyone in the family was enjoying harmony and closeness. This time, Jerry was happy to buy a lollipop for his little boy. The time after that, he came up with the idea of buying a lollipop with no prompting.

Naturally, Kelly had an easier time respecting Jerry when he was being generous, but they may have never gotten to that point if she hadn't been willing to uphold his decision when he said no.

MINIMIZE FAMILY CONFLICT BY MAXIMIZING RESPECT

Men show up for their roles as fathers in a completely different way once they feel respected by their wives. Even in cases where a man is verbally abusive to his children, there is much hope of the family being restored (as long as this is not accompanied by physical abuse, sexual abuse, or an active addiction). Children are less likely to be punished inappropriately, and more likely to be attended to generously when their father feels respected by his wife. Perhaps this is because kids are easy targets for misplaced anger. For example, if a man is angry with his wife for being bossy and domineering, he might try to keep the peace by saying nothing to her. In the meantime, the anger that was never properly vented seeps out as inappropriate outbursts at the children. This is terribly unfair, but it's also very human.

Since you've already identified him as one of the good guys, do your best not to interfere. This is simply another way of setting up a positive expectation for your husband to be a good father, and he knows best about that.

I have tremendous admiration for the mothers I know who have managed to surrender in parenting. Despite their "mama bear" instincts to protect their children at all costs, they never forget just how anxious their husbands are to protect their cubs, too. I've witnessed tremendous courage from these women, who clearly had to override this powerful protective instinct to respect the way their husbands play, handle crisis, and vent anger. In the long run, these women find themselves with husbands who are more dedicated, thoughtful fathers and more passionate, romantic lovers. Whether I'd be able to do this myself if I had children, I don't know, but my hat is off to the women who let their husband be the children's father.

18

LISTEN FOR THE HEART MESSAGE

> *"People need loving the most when they deserve it the least."*
> —John Harrigan

Spend one evening listening to your husband. Even if neither of you talks much, make a point of really hearing everything he says. Smile and invite him to say more by tilting your head and saying, "Really?" or "Oh?", then LISTEN. Acknowledge that you hear what your husband says (whether you agree with it or not) by saying, "I hear you."

When my husband got a higher-paying job a few years ago, he made a sarcastic comment that he hoped he was making enough money for me.

I felt surprised and hurt by his comment, but I didn't react. A few minutes later, I took this opportunity to tell him I was proud of him for getting this new job and that I felt well taken care of and happy. I was lucky that time because I was able to sort through the words and tone in his message to hear what he was really saying, which was that he wanted reassurance that I appreciated him.

Once I responded to what I call his "heart message," he perked up immediately, and I haven't heard a comment like that from him since.

A heart message is a statement that sounds like one thing on the surface, but means something else when you probe a little deeper. Your husband may not be explicit about his emotions, but you'll hear his vulnerability and truth in heart messages if you listen carefully. What you really want to know is the message that's hidden underneath your husband's words.

Often I don't realize that there's a message underneath my husband's words until I talk to someone else about what he said. Around here, heart messages are sometimes hidden under what sounds like a complaint. The romantic approach is to respond to these complaints by addressing the real message. Here are some examples of comments that have hidden heart messages:

MESSAGE: "Stop giving those kids everything they want!"
HEART MESSAGE: I want you to pay attention to me.

MESSAGE:	"No matter what I do around here, it's never enough for you!"
HEART MESSAGE:	I hope you appreciate me. I want you to notice what I do.
MESSAGE:	"There's no pleasing you, is there?"
HEART MESSAGE:	I'm afraid I don't make you happy. I hope I'm adequate as a husband.

As you can see, heart messages are difficult to hear and require some careful listening. Before I could even begin to hear these messages, however, I had to turn down my own volume, which I'll explain.

For so long, I thought that John needed to take more initiative and stop letting people walk all over him. I admonished, begged, manipulated, and cajoled him to speak up. I would make all the decisions, and then be annoyed that he wasn't communicating or expressing his ideas. I asked him a question, answered it myself, and then complained that I never knew what he was thinking and that he always seemed indifferent.

Ironically, as soon as I was willing to stop speaking up about everything, I started to hear John expressing his views and desires. Imagine my surprise when I discovered the problem wasn't apathy on his part, but that I just couldn't hear him—that he probably couldn't even hear himself—over my constant chatter.

In effect, I had silenced John. He was never louder than I was, so I could rarely hear him. It wasn't until I turned down my volume that I started to notice he was making any sounds at all. In retrospect, this makes perfect sense. Once John realized that his words fell on deaf ears, he stopped offering them. What was the point of his saying anything when I was so sure that I had a better idea, and signaled that I didn't see the point in listening to his?

THE BEST CONVERSATIONALISTS ARE LISTENERS

"A man is already halfway in love with any woman who
listens to him."
— BRENDAN FRANCIS

So how do you turn down the volume? I use a lot of duct tape to keep things from coming out of my mouth that I'll later wish I hadn't said.

For instance, one evening my husband and I were both reading at home when I interrupted him to ask how many years it would be until we would retire. He snapped back that this wasn't the appropriate time to talk about it. I was stunned by this response, and so sat there silently for a few minutes, trying to think up clever, hurtful retorts. Before I could say anything though, he looked up and said, "I'm sorry I snapped at you, but I'm worried that I haven't put anything into our retirement account in a long time. I guess I don't want to think about how that's going to affect us when we retire."

Good thing I was slow on the comeback. I would have missed getting an apology and started World War III. As it was, I got lucky. I hadn't yet thought of my retort, so I ended up serendipitously giving him space to talk before I jumped down his throat. That's how I discovered the gifts that come when I don't run in to fill the quiet space.

At least a few times a day, hold your tongue when you would normally speak, just to create a vacuum (a spot someone will naturally want to fill in with conversation) in the discussion. To better understand this, think about whether there's room for new furniture in your living room. If it's filled with the old furniture, then you need to create the space for a new couch by taking the old one to the dump first. Then you would have a vacuum, an empty space longing for furniture, where the old couch used to be. Being quiet in your relationship is the equivalent of dumping the couch before you have any idea where the new couch is going to come from. It leaves a space for something interesting and unexpected to come in.

In other words, be quiet.

Listen for what comes out of your husband when you are silent. Listening is a vital key to emotional connection that women frequently overlook. If you think your husband doesn't have much to say, has no ideas of his own or just sits there like a bump on a log, it could be that he never gets a word in edgewise. If you find him uncaring and indifferent to what the family needs, perhaps you aren't quiet long enough to hear him.

GOOD LISTENERS LET YOU KNOW THEY HEARD YOU

> *"Sometimes it is a great joy just to listen to someone we love talking."*
> —VINCENT MCNABB

Most people love to hear themselves talk, but if you're longing to hear him too, you need to be a good listener, which means that in a conversation, you demonstrate that you are truly taking in what is being said, not just thinking of what you're going to declare next. The first step in developing listening skills is to remember to take a break from talking every so often. Encourage him to speak by making eye contact, staying quiet, and asking questions whenever appropriate. But don't bombard him with inquiries because that can seem invasive.

A good listener acknowledges that she has heard what someone else said, and can do so without recounting her own story about a similar experience or giving advice. One of the ways I do this is by using the phrase, "I hear you." That assures my husband that I'm listening, and reminds me that I don't necessarily need to comment or advise him.

When you avoid interrupting your husband you will also become a better listener. To do this, make a point of waiting until he is done speaking, then count to three silently before you respond. This is also a great way to demonstrate that you are listening, rather than plotting your next sentence.

My friend Leah, who worked in sales for years, told me that people will gladly open up if you use the right body language. To encourage this, she tilted her head to the side a bit and raised one eyebrow occasionally and said nothing more than, "Oh?" It was amazing to me how Leah could get people to reveal themselves.

I knew another woman who was trying to get her teenage son to talk about his life. The more she questioned him, the tighter he seemed to clam up. Finally, she decided to give him the opportunity to speak to her without interrogating him, by silently preparing dinner at the kitchen table when he came home from school. Sure enough, her son came and sat down at the table too, and started telling her about his friends and what had happened at lunch that day. This wise woman knew enough to just listen without critical comment or interrogation, and she got a rare glimpse into her son's life.

The same approach will work for you in drawing your husband out. Just start by giving him space. You don't really even need to ask many questions. He may not tell you his feelings per se, but your husband will tell you about what's important to him, and in those words you will hear the heart messages. When you listen so well that you can hear the heart messages, you can be sure that intimacy will naturally follow. You can't help but connect with someone you know so well, nor can he help but feel affection for someone who really hears him.

THE GIFT OF GRANTING HIM SOME AIRTIME

The first duty of love is to listen.
— PAUL TILLICH

There are many conversations where using the words "I hear you" can be a tremendous gift. For instance, Shannon's husband started talking about how he wanted to retire on a ranch one day. Because she had tried to discourage him from wanting to buy such a large piece of property in the past, he looked at her and said somewhat defensively, "I'm just talking—it's just an idea!"

To acknowledge that she had heard him without passing any judgment on what he was saying, she simply smiled and said, "I hear you." After that, he talked to her about his vision in great detail, and she felt an emotional closeness with him that she hadn't felt in a long time. He revealed a part of himself that she hadn't seen—hadn't allowed, really—since they were first married. Hearing him talk about his fantasy of training horses and having a dog that followed him everywhere reminded Shannon of all that she found endearing and charming about her man. After a dozen years of marriage, Shannon was seeing a side to her husband as if for the first time—a part of him that wanted a simpler, quieter life.

One woman complained that her husband would follow her around the house when she was trying to do things. Then it occurred to her that he was trying to talk to her. Another woman noticed that she interrupted her husband every few minutes by jumping up to get the laundry, talking to her toddler, or answering the phone. Still another wife caught herself asking her husband questions, then tuning him out as soon as he began to answer. Pay special attention to how often your husband tries to talk to you—and to how you respond. Again, being conscious of your reactions will help you learn about him.

As an experiment, I went out to dinner with my husband and tried just listening—not talking about myself—for the whole meal. It wasn't easy. He had plenty of interesting things to say, but I kept getting distracted and thinking of what I wanted to tell him. I had to make a sincere attempt to keep listening. I wondered if he would ask me why I was so quiet, but he didn't. He probably didn't want to ruin his one chance of getting some airtime.

19

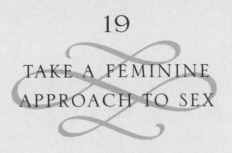

TAKE A FEMININE
APPROACH TO SEX

> *"You Jane. Me Tarzan."*
> — TARZAN

Think of the distinct differences between a man and a woman as gender contrast. Opposites really do attract, so the higher the contrast, the greater the magnetism between the couple. The more feminine you are, the more masculine your husband will be. For greatest attraction, set your contrast to high.

To do this be as feminine as possible when you're together. Make an effort to be soft, gentle, delicate, and receptive. The more you act like the woman you are, the sexier you'll feel and the more attractive you'll be to your man.

Instead of saying "let's have sex" or "we haven't had sex in two weeks," seduce your husband with your manner, your scent, your body, and your voice. There are lots of ways to let him know you're interested without putting a demand on him, so find the ones that work for you and use them when you're in the mood.

*H*igh gender contrast in a marriage is what makes things exciting in the bedroom. It means that instead of striving for agreement and sameness, you highlight and appreciate each other's unique characteristics and special traits. Just as we can't see stars without the cover of darkness, so the grandeur of our husband's masculinity is obscured without the foil of our femininity. By being feminine, we allow our husband's masculinity to shine. There can be no yin without yang, but the two together are sweet fulfillment—especially when it comes to sex.

Controlling wives are usually in charge of the contrast knobs because we have taken on so many masculine characteristics that our gender contrast is typically set very low. Your husband will respond to you with low contrast too, so that he matches you. That means he's going to be less attractive to you because he'll seem more feminine. For years we've said that we want men to be more sensitive, but as soon as they start talking about their feelings, we're not as attracted to them. I tell men not to fall for this trap, because what women typically want is a manly man—someone with his gender contrast set high. Of course the best way to have that is to adjust your own setting. He'll adjust his to match soon enough.

Most couples start their relationship with plenty of gender contrast, which is part of the reason that sex is so exciting initially. But then not only does the novelty wear off, the gender contrast diminishes as you become more sexually aggressive (a masculine characteristic) and he takes less sexual initiative (a feminine characteristic). Suddenly, even reruns of *Gilligan's Island* are more appealing than lovemaking.

Your physical union will intensify and have greater drama when you set your gender contrast to high. Just as our bodies are perfectly and intricately designed to fit together and bring each other pleasure, a feminine and masculine spirit complement each other brilliantly. Since you're the woman, come to the bedroom as female as possible. That means being soft, delicate, and receptive. Wearing something feminine never hurts either. It also means pretending that you never knew the meaning of ambition, aggression, or . . . control. It means that instead of being the aggressor in sex, you are the seductress.

Remember that we're more attractive to our husbands when we're soft, tender, vulnerable and receptive, since those qualities are fundamental to the nature of a woman. Your husband married a woman because it's women—in body, mind, and spirit—who turn him on.

A DEMAND IS A DEMAND

*I*n my own marriage, I made the mistake of telling my husband that I didn't think we were making love enough and that I wanted him to initiate it more. Without missing a beat, John told me he would add "have sex with Laura" to his list of chores—right between "take out the trash" and "weed the garden." Clearly he felt I was making a demand for him to perform, and he didn't like it. As you can imagine, this did absolutely nothing to enhance our sex life.

Next, I decided that I would simply take matters into my own hands by saying "let's have sex" when the moment seemed right. Another strikeout. John saw my strategy for what it was—simply another attempt to control an aspect of our marriage. Not surprisingly, John was increasingly reluctant and disinterested.

I had thought that making demands for sex (which all men crave, right?) was different from telling him to make the bed or watch my nephew while my sister and I had lunch. But the truth is, a demand is a demand.

Announcing that I wanted to have sex now created a miserable domino effect. I preferred to be aggressive because I felt more in control, but John was completely turned off. When he didn't respond enthusiastically, I was hurt and couldn't figure out why he wasn't interested in me. In my hurt, I was less likely to engage in any flirting, playing, or sexual teasing with him, which made the possibility of getting together even more remote.

Finally, out of sheer desperation I decided I would focus strictly on receiving from him, and that I wouldn't ask about sex. Besides, I actually preferred that John pursue me, because it made me feel sexy and irresistible. Without saying a word, I decided that rather than dragging him to me, I would strive to attract John.

As my more feminine approach sunk in, things began to shift in our relationship. Eventually, my husband noticed I was no longer making explicit or subtle demands for sex. He started to initiate lovemaking more, and as he did, I realized why I was so invested in controlling our sex life. I felt afraid of losing my cool exterior by responding to primitive pleasures. Just receiving and responding to my instincts left me feeling precarious. I wanted to know what was going to happen before it happened in order to feel safe. I couldn't handle spontaneous sex.

Now I realize he prefers to pursue me, and to see the very thing I tried to hide with control—my vulnerability. I'm simply more attractive to him now that I'm the coy target of his affection. Now I feel anticipation and excitement where I used to feel fear. Those were missing when I tried to start things by announcing it was time to do it.

SEVEN WAYS TO GET THE BALL ROLLING

"I love the idea of there being two sexes, don't you?"
— JAMES THURBER

The women in the Surrendered Circle had similar experiences with initiating sex. Still, none of us wanted just to sit and wait for our husbands to come to us if we were feeling amorous. So we thought of other ways to get the ball rolling when we were in the mood . . . without making demands or requests. The solution? We decided to show him we were available to receive sexually. There are hundreds of ways to do that, each with a varying degree of risk. Here are some examples:

1) Squeeze his arm and say "Oooh, you're strong."
2) Put on a negligee and lay on the bed with a book.
3) Tell him he looks sexy in those jeans and squeeze his butt.
4) Give him a long, slow kiss and a hug.
5) Snuggle up with him in bed.
6) Tell him that you're feeling especially erotic today.
7) Take off all your clothes and get into the bed or the shower with him.

SHOWING IS ALWAYS MORE POWERFUL
THAN TELLING

Telling your husband you think the two of you should have more sex is much less scary than making yourself available, of course, because with the former, you avoid really putting yourself out there where you could be rejected. Even if he says no, you won't feel much of anything because you have your armor on.

On the other hand, once you're laying on the bed in front of him in a lacy teddy and your intentions are unmistakable, anything short of an enthusiastic response will be disappointing. That's the vulnerability of receiving, instead of initiating. Because of these inherent risks, it may be tempting to read the obituaries or search the Internet for a bargain on vitamins instead of making yourself available.

When I surrendered sexually, I did the best I could to keep breathing and remember that I was with a man who loved me and wanted me to be happy. I told myself that I was safe and I focused on enjoying being pursued and desired. I admit, this tested my surrender limits, but I am also proud to report that my new behavior was blissfully rewarded.

If your husband responds enthusiastically when he sees that you're available, you will get what you wanted in the first place— sexual intimacy with your husband. That can be scary too, because true physical intimacy brings both partners to a very vulnerable state. But the more vulnerable you are, the more potential there is for passion, and that will take you on a journey to intense connection and satisfaction.

IMPROVE YOUR AVAILABILITY WITH SELF-CARE

> *"It's great to work with somebody who wants to do things differently."*
> — KEITH BELLOWS

But what if your husband is not approaching you as much as you might like? Patty's story illustrates the importance of staying focused on our own self-care in this situation instead of trying to manipulate or make demands.

One evening when Patty's husband came home from work, she found herself wishing he would approach her to make love. She also knew that she was just too tired to put energy into seducing him. Instead of saying anything, she asked herself what it was she needed right then. The answer was a nap, and she announced that she was going to lie down for a while. When she woke up two hours later, her husband had put the kids to bed and washed the dishes. Patty felt refreshed and grateful. When her husband came to bed shortly thereafter, he wanted to have sex with her, and everyone went to bed happy.

Had Patty not taken the nap, she would have felt tired and less available. Had she asked for sex, her husband might have felt controlled and resentful. The moral of the story is, as with all surrendering, to put your own needs first and let go of the results.

20

SAY YES
TO SEX

> *"That's enough, and enough is too much!"*
> — Popeye

Your marriage contract includes an agreement to have
a mutually exclusive sexual relationship, and you owe it
to your marriage to manifest your intimacy physically and
to keep your end of the bargain.

Make yourself available for sex at least once a week
whether you feel like it or not.

If you find yourself thinking of sex as a hassle or trying
to avoid it, ask yourself what you need to get in the
mood, and remember, as with all surrendering, express
your desires to your husband. Surrendering sexually
means you do your part to maintain a healthy sexual
relationship by regularly making yourself available for
this pleasurable experience.

*R*are is the marriage where both partners are completely satisfied with the frequency of sex. In *Annie Hall,* Woody Allen's character complains to his therapist that he and his wife hardly ever do it—only two, maybe three times a week. At the same time, she is complaining to her therapist that they do it all the time—two, maybe three times a week!

Sex in a marriage is one of the most spiritual ways that we remind ourselves who we are. Something mystical and inexplicable happens when couples bring their energy together and merge physically.

Surrendering in your marriage has a terrific effect in the bedroom, just as surrendering in the bedroom has a tremendous effect on your marriage. There are a few reasons for this. For one thing, men don't want to have sex with their mothers, and that's who we remind them of when we're controlling and bossy. For another thing, when a wife relinquishes control of when, how, and where sex happens, she is free to focus on receiving and being vulnerable. In response to this, the man's masculinity awakens and he feels more inclined to be tender and generous with his wife. The more attention he gives her, the more likely she will feel grateful and satisfied. If she expresses this gratitude, the man feels appreciated and is likely to give even more.

If you're thinking this sounds great in theory, but has nothing to do with your reality, take heart. This passionate, mutually gratifying sexual relationship isn't as elusive as you might think.

Since a healthy adult sexual response includes the desire to have sex, if you don't enjoy and look forward to making love with your husband, something's wrong. Just as you would suspect you were sick if you lost your appetite for food, losing your sexual appetite is an indication that all is not well, and you will want to do whatever you can to heal. You'll know when you're better because your desire will return in full swing.

Perhaps a drop in your sex drive means you're resentful or angry. Maybe something physical is turning you off. You might have an emotional injury that interferes with your normal desires. Whatever the root of the problem, curing it is critical to intimacy. Here are some of the underlying reasons women lose interest in sex.

THE COMMON COMPLAINTS

"The definition of a beautiful woman is one who loves me."
—SLOAN WILSON

"I'm Not in the Mood."

I often hear women say that they are "not in the mood." This is *not* a wise reason to refuse your husband in bed. Moods come and go, and, as you know, just because you don't start out wanting to have sex doesn't mean you won't end up there before it's over.

You always have a choice about what to do with your body. But if it's intimacy you're after, say "yes" at least once a week when your husband wants to make love regardless of whether you're in the mood. After all, why would you pass up the chance to have physical intimacy with your husband when it's such a vital part of overall intimacy? Agreeing to make love with your husband helps make him feel loved.

This is not to say that you should be a doormat. Agreeing to have sex doesn't mean you don't ask for what you want first. For instance, I might respond to my husband's advances by saying "I'd love a back rub to get me in the mood," or "I'm up for it, but only if you can catch me first." I might request candles and scented oil, a certain sex position or an old Steely Dan album first. Generally he's more than happy to give me what I want because, as always, he wants to make me happy.

"I Don't Feel Emotionally Connected with Him."

If you've lost your appetite for sex because you feel abandoned in your marriage and overwhelmed with all your responsibilities, it may be that you're exhausted from doing everything, or can't find the time to get romantic after working and taking care of kids all day. Remember that as you begin to relinquish some responsibilities to your husband, you'll have more energy, so part of the cure is to practice the other steps of surrendering—being respectful, receiving graciously, relinquishing control, expressing gratitude, and (perhaps most of all) practicing good self-care. As you commit to regular physical contact, you will begin to find more enjoyment in it because you can devote the energy you were formerly using to avoid sex to expressing what you want to make sex enjoyable for you. Who knows? Maybe lovemaking will make your list of the top ten things you love to do.

If you're thinking, "He doesn't do anything to help me, so why should I do something he wants?" remember that everybody loses during a long, lonely standoff. This attitude puts you no closer to restored harmony. Not least of all, withholding sex as a bargaining chip in the relationship is a terrible misuse of physical intimacy. If you make sex seem like a reward for "good" behavior rather than a mutual pleasure, you abuse your power and dismiss your own healthy desires. Saying yes whenever you can is a good way to ensure that you avoid the chilling effect of a sexual power struggle.

"I Can't Get Aroused."

Even if you don't feel irritated with or estranged from your husband there could still be another reason you're feeling disconnected from your desire in general. Check with your doctor to see if there's a physical cause. Certain medications can lower your libido. Nursing a baby or going through menopause may also cause you to feel temporarily disinterested in sex. Sometimes there are simple solutions to these hindrances, such as switching to a different medication or employing a hormone therapy.

If the doctor says there's nothing to do about your diminished desire but wait (to stop nursing, to complete the medication, or to advance to the next stage of menopause, for instance), make yourself available at least once a week anyway. Assuming you're not going to experience pain, this is really not that much different than not being in the mood. If you don't show up for sex, you will still cheat yourself (and your husband) out of an intimate physical connection. If you do show up—who knows? By the end you may be enjoying yourself too. Remember to speak up about what will make it enjoyable for you.

IDENTIFYING AND HEALING A SEXUAL INJURY

"Perfect love is rare indeed—for to be a lover will require that you continually have the subtlety of the very wise, the flexibility of the child, the sensitivity of the artist, the understanding of the philosopher, the acceptance of the saint, the tolerance of the scholar and the fortitude of the certain."
— LEO BUSCAGLIA

*I*f you're experiencing a tremendous amount of fear as you're reading this, perhaps you are avoiding sex to protect yourself from feeling the pain of a previous sexual injury. If that's the case, you're not alone.

I have also felt ambivalent about making love with my husband. I always wanted to enjoy a physical relationship, but another part of me didn't want sex at all. When I started discussing my ambivalence honestly with other women, I noticed we had something in common: Many of us had suffered some kind of emotional injury related to sex and we were haunted by a lingering sense of powerlessness and violation.

Some women had engaged sexually when they were too young, while others were the victims of rape, incest, or molestation. Regardless of the trauma, the travesty was the same: We sometimes associated sexual experiences with our earlier injuries, and could feel tremendous anxiety even during a healthy, consensual sexual encounter.

Simply put, we were fearful of not having control of our bodies.

We preferred to control when, where, and how to make love, because it somehow felt safer, which makes perfect sense since control comes from fear. We all said we wanted to be pursued, but then when we were, we often turned our husbands down. This prevented us from experiencing the pleasure of spontaneous sex with our partners. Our old defense kept us from connecting and left us feeling lonely.

If you sometimes feel obligation or pressure to perform when your husband initiates lovemaking, you may have a sexual injury. If you're thinking that you *always* feel pressured to perform when your husband approaches you sexually, take a look at the underlying fear. This fear and sense of obligation manifests itself as a reluctance to engage in any physical contact at all. The reasoning goes something like this:

1) If I kiss him, he might get turned on.
2) If he gets turned on, he'll want to have sex with me.
3) If he wants to have sex with me, I'll have to because I got him aroused in the first place.
4) I may not want to have sex with him, so if I want to keep my options open . . .
5) I won't kiss him—at least, not like that!

The problem with this thinking is that it also prevents us from engaging in sensual activities that don't necessarily culminate in an orgasm. Erotic pleasures like back rubs, showering together, or just being playful seem too threatening to enjoy.

If you identify with having sexual injuries, you may want to find a gentle, safe counselor who can support you in processing your experiences and helping you heal. You may even need to take a break from having sex with your husband while you're opening up the wounds and trying to heal them.

But didn't you just say I should always say yes?

I did, as a matter of fact, but I'm making an exception. If you are working with a therapist or are engaging in some other form of healing, it may be necessary to take a temporary break.

Let your husband know that you're working on some issues of your own that may make you unavailable for sex, but put a time limit on it—say three months. Promise that you'll let him know when you're available again. Thank him for bearing with you. Assure him that you still think he's attractive and that the injuries you're healing have nothing to do with him. He might continue to approach you in the meantime, and in each moment you will get to decide if you're available.

Just communicating about your lack of desire will help to improve the intimacy in your relationship. Instead of wondering if you'll ever be a willing sex partner, your man will have hope for the future. Also, asking your husband to support you in a situation like this taps into his masculine instinct to protect you.

If you're thinking that your husband will not respond supportively, consider Gina's experience.

She told her husband that she was working on some sexual injuries that she endured as a teenager, and that she wouldn't be available for a few months while she dealt with them. Gina was so nervous telling her husband this that she could only look at the ground and try to keep from shaking. But once the words were out, she was relieved and rewarded. Her husband responded like the tender, good guy he is and said he loved her—no matter what—and wanted to protect her. When Gina asked her husband if he would bear with her for a while he said, "Of course, I will."

You will probably be pleasantly surprised too because telling your husband about the fears you have surrounding sexuality makes you vulnerable. It demonstrates a degree of trust and faith in your husband that he will want to honor. When you reveal yourself he will not only want to protect you, he will also find you beautiful.

Now that you have his support I urge you to seek help from a therapist, an online or community support group, or a book such as *The Courage to Heal: A Guide for Women Survivors of Child Sexual Abuse* by Laura Davis. Do whatever you have to do to heal so you can be sexually whole. Just as your appetite returns when you're over the flu, your desire to be desired will return as you heal sexually. You need only be tender and reassuring with yourself while you're healing to discover it again.

THE SEVEN SEXUAL MYTHS

"Oh, I'm scared all the time! I just act as if I'm not."
— KATHARINE HEPBURN

If you suffer from a sexual injury you may subscribe to common misconceptions that make you feel obligated—and therefore pressured—to be sexual. Here are some of the common myths—and the lesser-known facts—that I've heard from the women I know.

1. Myth: *If I don't have sex with him, he'll look for it someplace else.*

Fact: If your husband is one of the good guys, you have nothing to worry about. In other words, if he's not a sex addict who is sleeping with other women, you will not drive a healthy man to seek sex elsewhere by taking a temporary sexual healing break. (If he is a sex addict acting out with other women, see the section in the introduction called "When Not to Surrender and Get Out.")

If your husband has a history of infidelity it will be harder to believe that he will remain faithful while you're not temporarily available. But, if he has the capacity to be faithful, he can certainly go without sex on occasion. He cannot, however, live without respect and admiration. Ongoing control and criticism are far more dangerous threats to monogamy than the absence of sex.

If you can't be sexual with him right now, your husband does deserve the promise of sex in the future. Let's say you decide to work with a therapist to heal some old wounds, and during that time the pain is so intense that you decide to tell your husband you won't be sexually available for three months or so. If you talk openly with him about not being available and that the situation is temporary, it's very unlikely that he'll look for sex someplace else during a short-lived break.

It's true that men have been known to cheat on their wives out of anger and loneliness. However, it's usually a last resort for regaining the masculinity and intimacy that are lost when he's lived with ongoing criticism and control. Another motivation for a man to cheat on his wife is the feeling that he may *never* get his sexual needs met in his marriage. While neither of these situations would make his cheating your fault (he is always responsible for honoring his wedding vows), it only makes sense to avoid emasculating him or withholding sex indefinitely.

When you acknowledge that a healthy sex life is important to you, and that you plan to return to one as soon as possible, you are fostering intimacy and trust in your marriage. That's very different from just ignoring his frustration and making no commitments to improve in the future.

Your husband may very well need more sex than you are able to offer him if you're unavailable for a while. Fortunately, men know exactly how to satisfy themselves when we're not available. Your husband probably went many months or years without sex plenty of times before he met you. A hiatus with you is not going to drive him into some other woman's bed. Remind yourself of this when you feel afraid.

Some women feel threatened when their husbands masturbate, but men tend to view masturbating as a bodily function, rather than a cataclysmic sexual experience. According to the old joke, 98 percent of all men masturbate and the other 2 percent lie. Your husband is probably like most men. He may even use pornography when he masturbates. But what he's reading or watching is strictly between him and God, and it's none of your business. A centerfold is not the same as a flesh-and-bones woman, so don't make it more than it is.

You may find these views on the topics of masturbation and pornography distasteful, but keep in mind that you can't control your husband's masturbating or pornography viewing. Trying to stop him is a form of controlling—which wastes your time and interferes with your intimacy. Remember that part of the reason he's attracted to you is because he's attracted to the female form. That's the way he's made.

2. Myth: *"If I have sex with him, I'll have to work hard to prevent him from seeing how fat/freckled/wrinkled/sweaty I am."*

Fact: We're accustomed to thinking that we're unattractive if we haven't showered, done our hair, put on makeup and perfume, or put on a pretty outfit with matching earrings. We women are especially hard on ourselves when it comes to the way we look. But no matter what your state, you have a womanly shape and scent and a feminine spirit that is attractive to your man, which is why he's making goo-goo eyes. Seize that opportunity to connect.

Try not to flinch if your husband fondles your stomach, looks at your thighs, or runs his fingers through your dirty hair. Don't stand between him and what he finds pleasurable. Don't worry about how you smell or what bodily fluids you've excreted. If he doesn't care, why should you? Being overly self-conscious is a barrier to intimacy. When you accept yourself as you are, you will even start to feel attractive at times that you never thought you would.

If you refuse him because you insist that you are not attractive, you're acting on the belief that this man has bad taste, when clearly he has excellent taste as evidenced by the fact that he married you. You are also criticizing what he thinks, which is disrespectful and ungracious.

Passing up an opportunity to have a physically intimate moment with your husband because you feel inadequate is unpleasant for everybody. You're denying him the chance to give you pleasure and yourself the chance to receive it and feel beautiful in his arms all because you feel insecure about your body. Why not use the opportunity to feel great? Tell yourself, "I turn him on! He must think I am sexy and gorgeous." Even if he's not telling you so in words, notice what his actions are saying.

3. Myth: *"If I don't have sex with him now, he won't approach me again."*

Fact: While it's true that repeated rejections can be discouraging, it's not likely to make your husband stop trying. Just as people keep tugging at the lever of a slot machine, so your husband is also optimistic about hitting the jackpot. This is especially true if you have told your husband up front that you might not be available and that it's not about him, because then he won't take your rejection personally. Another reason he won't stop trying is that part of his physical makeup drives him to mate with you. His instincts tell him to plant his seed.

If your husband is not approaching you, a much more significant problem may be rejection outside the bedroom. Keep working on respecting and deferring to him. And, of course, practice making yourself available.

4. Myth: *"If I don't have sex with him when he wants to, he won't love me."*

Fact: His love for you doesn't depend on sex. You are lovable whether you are performing sexually or not, and to believe otherwise reflects a painful lack of self-worth. Don't discount the unique qualities that made your husband fall in love with you in the first place. Your husband loves you for lots of reasons—the way you mother his children, make a home, laugh at his jokes, know the names of all the constellations, admire his muscles, or wear your hair when you're going to the beach. Remind yourself that you have intrinsic value as a person, not just as a sex partner. Your husband did not marry you just for the sex. For that, he could have made arrangements that required much less effort on his part.

A reasonable man will not insist on having sex when you're unavailable. He may complain loudly, but he won't stop loving you because you're abstaining for a little while. Keep in mind that he wants you to be happy, and if that means entertaining himself for the moment, so be it.

5. Myth: *"If I have sex with him and it's only so-so, he'll complain that it's not as good as it used to be."*

Fact: You might end up having terrific sex when you least expect it. Remember that the point of lovemaking is to connect physically and to distinguish your marriage from every other relationship. Not all sex is fabulous, so don't hold yourself to an impossible standard.

6. Myth: *"If I don't have sex with him, he'll be angry and I will feel guilty."*

Fact: This may be true.

But there's a simple antidote for not keeping your sexual agreement. Apologize. Acknowledge that you have deprived him sexually, and tell him you are doing everything you can to get to the root of the problem and heal it so you'll be available for him.

You can't afford to feel guilty or be harsh with yourself.

It's appropriate that you feel remorse, and that you try to speed the process of renewing intimacy by making an effort to be available to your husband. However, guilt only robs you of the energy you'll need to address the issues that stand between you and a pleasurable sex life.

7. Myth: *"If I start to have sex with him, I'll have to satisfy him to the point of orgasm."*

Fact: Women with sexual abuse in their past especially tend to feel this way, and understandably so. If you've survived a rape, date rape, or molestation, you probably identify with this belief, and you have internalized the idea that "no" is not an option.

Some wives had an overly simplistic, black-and-white view of sex that made us feel we were either going to do it and go all the way, or we weren't going to engage at all. Once we acquiesced to a kiss, or got undressed or passed some other symbolic starting point, there was no turning back.

If your husband is one of the good guys as described in the first chapter, then he is not one of the creeps who forced you. Remind yourself that he never will be. If you ask a good guy (i.e., your husband) to stop in the middle of lovemaking, he may protest, but he won't rape you. I asked the women in the circle to do this as a one-time experiment, and I recommend it for you too, to demonstrate that you are in charge of your body. Once we had the proof, we knew that we could always choose. That made it easier to say yes more often, and have the physical intimacy we craved. The truth is, you always have a choice, and knowing that will make you feel freer to engage in lovemaking.

* * *

I have talked to hundreds of women, and among those who have a lack of desire for sex, the majority subscribe to the seven myths. Too many have a history of sexual abuse.

In other words, you are not alone. But you need to take responsibility for your own healing, particularly if you've been blaming your husband for your lack of desire. For instance, some women complain to me that their husbands always want sex from them—as if that's a problem. They're surprised when I say "That's great!" As I see it, his actions prove that he has a healthy male sex drive, he doesn't see her as his mother and he's physically attracted to her, all of which is good news.

It takes tremendous courage to heal from sexual wounding, but if the women in the first Surrendered Circle could find that courage, so can you. You deserve to have the freedom to enjoy your own sexuality with the man who has committed to you for life, so don't let your fear and old wounds stand in your way. You'll never feel more feminine, or him more masculine, than when you're enjoying the zenith of physical intimacy with the love of your life.

21
NEVER
EAT WORMS

How unhappy is he who cannot forgive himself.
—PUBLILIUS SYRUS

Every time you start thinking up insults for yourself about how difficult you are to live with, how awful you've been to your husband, or what a terrible job you're doing with surrendering, stop and replace the thoughts with a compliment for yourself.

Just as you wouldn't scream at a child who stumbles as he learns to walk, don't be harsh with yourself as you learn to surrender. Instead, acknowledge your progress and offer yourself some encouragement.

*W*hen I first started surrendering, I suddenly became aware of all the things I did that I wished I didn't do—but I couldn't change my behavior so immediately. It made me feel so rotten that I was tempted to go out and eat some worms to punish myself. I call this Worm Syndrome. If you can't stop controlling your husband perfectly (and nobody can), every time you slip, you feel shame on top of your sadness.

Here's an analogy: Let's say that you discover that you're dairy intolerant, which is causing you discomfort. Upon hearing this news, you resolve to give up milk, cheese, and ice cream to prevent indigestion, even though these are your favorite things.

The next day you get up and, out of habit, make yourself a bowl of cereal and milk. Then, just as you're about to take the first bite, you remember that you were going to give up drinking milk. With a bite of your favorite, comforting breakfast just inches from your mouth, you decide to postpone your resolution for one more day. But as you crunch the cereal and slurp the sweet milk, something is different. With each bite a twinge of self-recrimination comes over you. "I'm making myself feel sick!" you moan to yourself. You tell yourself you really should stop and stop now, but you can't. At least, not yet.

Now your misery is complete. You are indulging in your old eating habits, but you can't even enjoy them because you feel guilty. You have the new information, but you can't apply it yet. You will have no peace until you either give up dairy products, or decide to find some other solution to your problem.

It's the same with surrendering. Seeing the road ahead paved with intimacy does not necessarily give you the courage to drive down it autobahn-style right away. Instead, you merely recognize when you're being disrespectful at first, and wince each time you remember you were going to stop doing that.

Nobody surrenders perfectly—or even very well at first. Still, recognizing your behavior and having the information to take a stab at changing it *is* progress. It only feels like torture because every time you're disrespectful, critical, demeaning, or dismissing, a huge billboard lights up in your brain and says, "See!?! You're doing it again!!!" Some of us also inwardly scream insults at ourselves like:

"Why would anyone want to be married to you!"

"You are a terrible wife!"

"You are absolute hell to live with!"

When you hear things like this in your head, remember that you're inner voice is *wrong*.

Your husband wants to be married to you or he would have left long ago. A terrible wife would never embark on the surrendering process at all. And telling yourself that you are hell to live with discounts all your wonderful qualities. Surrendering is just as much about feeling good about the woman and wife you are as it is about reintroducing intimacy to your marriage, so don't let the critical voices in your head tell you you're bad. It's simply not true.

As you practice surrendering, it becomes second nature, like any other habit. Your need to control diminishes. Your urge to criticize fades. Your sense of respect for your husband will become genuine. But still you won't be perfect.

There will be days when you get fed up or disgusted and lose it completely. Surrendering is not so different from other life habits. For instance, you may put your keys on the same hook every day so you don't lose them, but once in a while you forget and misplace them.

Life is not ideal. No good habit is fool-proof. Overall, you are going to be able to find your keys most of the time because they're on the hook. The same is true of surrendering. You will be better off, happier, more dignified and intimate, even if you don't surrender perfectly.

TURN UP THE POSITIVE VOICE IN YOUR HEAD

"There's always room for improvement, you know—it's the biggest room in the house."
—LOUISE HEATH LEBER

No matter how poorly you're doing, do not insult yourself. A lot of things get started in your head, and a negative inner dialogue can become a runaway train. When you insult yourself, apologize to yourself immediately. You might say something like: "I didn't mean that. You have lots of good qualities, like a terrific sense of humor (or whatever is true for you). You're making progress with surrendering, so good job! I don't expect you to be perfect."

Say this out loud, to give it a voice. This will probably feel entirely silly, but then again some people will think this whole concept of surrendering is ridiculous. So as long as you're going to be silly, you might as well be nice to yourself while you're doing it.

GIVE CREDIT WHERE CREDIT IS DUE

*"Any change, even a change for the better, is always
accompanied by drawbacks and discomforts."*
—ARNOLD BENNETT

*W*hen I tell some women to apologize to themselves, they try to explain that they *really aren't* doing a good job. They tell me they've taken one step forward but ten steps back. They tell me how completely rotten and horrible they've been.

If you have apologized to your husband for being disrespectful even once, withheld criticism even once, deferred to his thinking even once, let him solve his own problem even once, or expressed your gratitude for him even once, you have begun to surrender. Even if you raged at him and berated him and dismissed him ten times after that, you have begun to surrender.

Give yourself credit for what you have done right.

Acknowledge to yourself that you have taken action toward changing your life, and encourage yourself to try again tomorrow.

If you continue to surrender and to support yourself in your genuine efforts, tomorrow *will* be different. Don't clobber yourself every time you say something regrettable. Make apologies as appropriate and give yourself credit for changing according to your new insights. Think about how many people ignore new information because they are afraid of changing the *status quo* or because it's inconvenient. But you are heading directly into the intimidating waters of transformation. What courage you have!

Even if you have done nothing else, you have made progress

by getting this book. Give yourself a pat on the back, and keep reading.

MORE PITFALLS TO AVOID

"If we don't change, we don't grow. If we don't grow, we aren't really living."
—GAIL SHEEHY

*T*here's one more pitfall to watch out for. If you're like me, you will have a feeling of profound sadness when you compare your new behavior to your old habits. Once you begin surrendering even the tiniest little bit, you will begin to see the horror of your old self.

This happened to Margaret when she and her husband Glenn went to a Chinese restaurant that was partly self-service. They ordered at the counter and a server brought them their food, but they bussed their own trays on the way out, which is why Margaret had objected to leaving a tip on a previous visit, ages ago. After she started surrendering, Glenn brought up the idea of leaving a tip again. This time, she shrugged and said, "whatever you think," so Glenn left some money. Suddenly Margaret knew that each of the dozens of times they had been there before, Glenn had probably wanted to leave a tip, but he didn't because he feared Margaret's disapproval.

"Seeing with this new perspective, I feel awful about everything I had done before," she told me.

I felt the same way when I watched John quit a job he had

hated for four years only to land a higher-paying one that he liked better shortly after I surrendered. I knew he had hesitated to leave his job because of my worries about our financial security. I realized I had been discouraging him from making a change because of *my* fear.

Sure, our husbands could have done things differently if they really wanted to, but they would have done so against the wishes of the one person in the world who matters most to them. So it's pretty sad to see how you've been keeping your best friend and lover from pursuing those things—big and small—that would make him happy. But no matter how much you regret your behavior in the past, do not wallow in guilt about it now. That's an unproductive energy drain.

Sister Wendy Beckett, a well-known art critic and one of the wisest women on the planet, told Bill Moyers during an interview "I don't think being truly human has any place for guilt. . . . Contrition, yes, but guilt no. Contrition means you tell God you are sorry and you're not going to do it again and you start off afresh. All the damage you've done to yourself [is] put right. Guilt means you go on and on belaboring and having emotions and beating your breast and being ego-fixated. Guilt is a trap. People love guilt because they feel if they suffer enough guilt, they'll make up for what they've done, whereas, in fact, they're just sitting in a puddle and splashing. Contrition, you move forward. It's over. You are willing to forego the pleasure of guilt."

The next time you find yourself contemplating a big plate of worms, make a decision to forego the satisfaction of guilt.

22

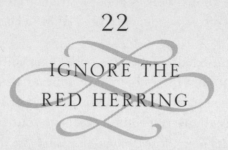

IGNORE THE
RED HERRING

*Husbands are awkward things to deal with; even keeping
them in hot water will not make them tender.*
—MARY BUCKLEY

*Let your urge to control be a clue that you need to
examine your feelings. When you find yourself thinking,
he's loading the dishwasher the wrong way, ask yourself
what's really bugging you right at that moment. Call a
friend, and keep talking until you figure it out, but don't
attack your husband.*

*Likewise, if you're going to tell your husband you are
angry or unhappy about something, first rehearse with a
friend how you will present your issue. Check to see if
you can deliver the message in terms of how hurt or sad
you feel, rather than angry. Practice delivering your
message so that you stick to the topic and don't throw in
red herrings that will detract from your legitimate issue.*

*I*n a detective story, the red herring is the misleading information that keeps the detective from discovering the truth. I have learned that my temptation to control John—whether it's wondering when he's going to start the taxes or how he's going to make it to work on time—is also a way to distract myself from figuring out what's nagging at me in my own life.

For example, maybe I'm nervous about my impending deadline or irritated with a client for not getting back to me. Perhaps I'm upset with a friend who has hurt my feelings, or I'm just plain exhausted. I sometimes try to displace my anxiety about these situations on my husband by trying to control him.

Now that I'm on to myself about this, I've learned to look inward when I think something my husband is doing is bugging me. Even if I can't put my finger on what I'm worried about, now I can eliminate whatever my husband is doing from the list of usual suspects.

Feeling powerless about a situation in your own life can sometimes lead to the urge to rearrange somebody else's. Other people's shortcomings are easier to see than our own, and their problems seem easier to fix since we have no attachment to them. Unfortunately, taking the approach of trying to "fix" your husband will not only impede intimacy, it will also irritate him. On top of that, it brings you no closer to solving your original problem.

When Sharon called to tell me that her husband was not spending enough time with their daughter, I sensed she was distracted by a red herring. She was sure that she had a legitimate gripe and was annoyed by the very suggestion that there could be something in her own life that she might feel anxious about. Finally, she admitted that she was sad and scared about talking to her sister, with whom she had been quarreling. This was a difficult topic for Sharon—and she wanted to avoid it. Focusing on her husband's shortcomings was a handy diversion.

While Sharon was avoiding the unpleasantness of dealing with her sister, she was creating another problem by criticizing her husband's behavior. He then wanted to avoid her. Now, she was lonely, wanted to eat worms, *and* she still wasn't talking to her sister.

The next time I spoke to Sharon, she had a different perspective. She saw that she had been distracted by a red herring—her husband's parenting—and needed to handle the real McCoy—the situation with her sister. Finally, she approached her sister and reached some resolution. Afterwards, she acknowledged that her husband was quite attentive to their daughter. The huge concern she'd had the other day seemed like an overreaction now. Her husband had been supportive in listening to her process the conflict with her sister; and she no longer had the urge to criticize him, or "let him have it" about his parenting.

IDENTIFYING THE REAL McCOY

> "If you are patient in one moment of anger, you will escape a hundred days of sorrow."
> —CHINESE PROVERB

*S*ometimes you'll have a legitimate complaint about your husband. Perhaps he is chronically late, sloppy, cranky, insulting, or smelly. Sometimes you will want to berate him for one of his truly annoying habits. But how can you tell the difference between a red herring and a situation where you need to speak up?

If you find yourself with a criticism about something that doesn't usually bother you, chances are it's a red herring. If you're thinking about something small (he doesn't rinse out his coffee cups and they're gross), it's most likely a red herring. His habit may truly bug you, but is it worth nipping him so he'll want to avoid you? No. Instead, ask yourself what could be bothering you. Are you overtired, hungry, or lacking in self-care? Try to give yourself what you need.

If, however, you find yourself with a complaint that eats at you repeatedly—and it's not that his socks never make it into the hamper—then you have something to talk about.

Once you eliminate other suspects and you're sure that you have an authentic problem with your husband, the first thing to do is to talk about it with another wife, preferably somebody who is supportive of your surrendered marriage. Tell this girlfriend how sad you feel that your husband hasn't approached you for sex in weeks, or that he belittled you again, or that you're tired of being broke all the time.

Your fear, sadness, hurt, and anger are real. Do not dismiss them. Do not try to pretend that they're not there. Express these feelings to yourself, your friends, or your therapist. If all else fails, write them down.

If you feel something, it's as real as this book that you're holding now. Before you decided to surrender to your husband, you may have expressed those feelings to him indiscriminately. Discussing your emotions with *someone* is good for your mental health. Blurting out your feelings—which may at times have been harsh or negative—to your husband is not ideal for your marriage. Those sharp words cause conflict and put distance between you and your spouse. Therefore, I'm suggesting that you seek validation for these feelings privately *outside* of your marriage.

In other words, don't squash your feelings. It won't work. I've tried to squash mine, but I am always reminded that feelings demand an outlet. You can't wish them away or dismiss them; the more you get to the heart of them the more you know about yourself and your marriage.

If you don't know any other wives who practice surrendering, get on the Internet and go to the bulletin board at www.surrenderedwife.com. Describe your situation and ask for support. You will find remarkable wisdom and compassion there.

EFFECTIVELY REGISTERING YOUR FEELINGS

> *"Rare is the person who can weigh the faults of others without his thumb on the scale."*
> — BYRON LANGFELD

Obviously, there will be times when you need to address your husband directly. But learning to communicate clearly will make your message ten times more effective. Start by separating the real issues from the red herrings. Since most controlling wives tend to err on the side of saying too much and end up diluting real issues with inappropriate rages, it's best to reason things out with someone else first. Rehearse what you are going to say so that it's focused, clear, and free of blame or shame. You certainly wouldn't want to let those red herrings obscure a valid point. If your complaint is legitimate, it can wait until you've discussed it with someone else. This is an important part of learning to communicate clearly. I struggle with this myself because when I'm exasperated, I don't want to wait for anything. I just want to let him have it!

Janet's husband, Danny, repeatedly made her late to choir practice by coming home behind schedule to take care of their son. She was so angry at his lack of consideration that she wanted to accuse him of never supporting her. According to Janet, he was so self-absorbed that he couldn't enjoy spending quality time alone with their child.

Fortunately, before Janet said anything, she talked to other women about the situation. She told her neighbor about her frustration, and in speaking about it, she realized that there was only one thing she was truly upset about: being late for choir practice. She couldn't claim that Danny didn't support her passion for the choir because he came to every performance. How could she say that he didn't love being with their son when she knew that he always looked forward to their pizza nights alone?

So, aided by the perspective she gained from conversations with women, Janet stayed focused. She delivered a pure message by saying "When you come home late on Tuesday nights, I feel disappointed that I have to be late to choir practice." Then she left for rehearsal without further discussion.

When she came home later that night, still feeling marvelous from all that harmonizing, Danny was brooding. He baited her a few times, looking for the comfort of a familiar brawl. But Janet felt too good to engage and simply rebuffed his self-critical comments that he was "such a loser" and "couldn't do anything right." Instead, she told him she appreciated him for providing her with the opportunity to participate in the choir. Her gratitude caught him off-guard and disarmed him. They went to bed without an argument.

The following week, he was home in plenty of time for Janet to make it to the start of choir practice. She thanked her husband for being so considerate.

If Janet had said, "You're always late and I'm sick of it!" or "Why don't you try being on time for a change!" her husband probably wouldn't have heard her feelings, much less taken them seriously. Instead, they would have been locked in a battle, and before either of them knew it, they would have lost the main issue— Janet's getting to practice on time—in the crossfire. But Janet's short, to-the-point comment left Danny to think about only one thing: his behavior. He seemed to feel the weight of what he'd done, since there weren't any distractions to help him tune out.

Janet had a legitimate issue, and by "picking her battle" carefully she avoided provoking a fight and going to bed in a huff. Instead, her husband heard her feelings in a mature, fair, and strong way. How could he not be attracted to that? No intimacy was lost, and everything was gained.

The same will happen for you when you process your complaints with a wise friend before you deliver a message to your husband.

23
RELY ON A
SPIRITUAL CONNECTION

"If a man does not keep pace with his companions, perhaps
it is because he hears a different drummer. Let him step to
the music which he hears, however measured or far away."
—HENRY DAVID THOREAU

Whatever your faith, trust that your husband is the
instrument of a higher being and make a decision to
appreciate what He has created.

Remember how miraculous it seemed to meet him and
fall in love and marry? Your husband's presence in your
life is no less miraculous today, so don't take it for
granted. Your higher power brought you together for an
important reason—so that you could grow into your best
selves. Remember that the challenges that your husband
presents are partly your lessons to learn.

*W*hen you have faith in a divine power, you have assurance that someone is watching over you. When you surrender to your husband, you accept that a supreme being is looking after you both, which gives you a safety net to keep surrendering even when you're terrified.

When you trust in a higher being, you acknowledge that things beyond *your* power are the way they are meant to be. You learn to yield your will, enjoy things just as they are, and exist in greater harmony, not just with your husband, but with all the circumstances in your life.

SURRENDERING IS A SPIRITUAL METAPHOR

> *We need to find God, and he cannot be found in noise and*
> *restlessness. God is the friend of silence. See how nature—*
> *trees, flowers, grass—grows in silence; see the stars, the*
> *moon and the sun, how they move in silence . . . We need*
> *silence to be able to touch souls.*
> — MOTHER TERESA

*H*arboring the illusion that you can control someone else is about as reasonable as believing that you can control the waves in the ocean—and just as frustrating. Letting go of that illusion is a spiritual journey. It is the process of learning reverence for the divine order of the universe, and acquiring the wisdom of acceptance. This journey requires faith in things unseen and acceptance that there are some things you simply can't change.

If you don't have a higher power or don't believe in one, surrendering to your husband is going to be a very tough leap. Without faith in a power greater than you, you might as well continue to try to control everyone and everything around you. After all, if you are the only one who's watching out for you, then it makes sense that you would try to control your circumstances as much as possible.

For example, if you are secure in the knowledge that your higher power is your source for all things, then when you have financial worries for your husband you can remind yourself that the Creator is in charge, and that everything will happen in perfect divine timing. If you find yourself wanting to correct your husband's parenting skills, you can act on the belief that God made your husband the father of your children for a reason, and that it's not your job to second-guess your husband or God. When you're tempted to criticize or teach your husband, you can remind yourself that he has his own higher power and you're not it. With a higher power running things, there's no reason to try to control your husband.

In fact, trying to control another person is as pointless and futile as trying to control the ocean, but just for the sake of argument, let's say you were going to try. You might tell the waves to calm down and the water to move back, but of course, nothing unusual would happen. You could then jump up and down and scream at the ocean to do as you say, but still nothing would change. You might even try to push the waves back with your hands, but you'd only get all wet. By this time, you would probably be agitated and stressed out, but no closer to getting the ocean to do what you tell it to do. (Does this remind you of trying to control your husband?) You certainly wouldn't have any peace.

Since you know you cannot reckon with the forces of nature, I'm sure you don't even try. When you're *not* trying to alter the waves, you're free to admire their extraordinary force and beauty. You can just relax and enjoy yourself. Allowing yourself to be nourished and energized—instead of depleted and frustrated—as you look at the ocean is a reminder that the Creator is far more powerful than you.

You can also take comfort in knowing that God manages impeccably without your help. Focusing on the beauty of the water meeting the sand might help you remember that although you cannot see the Creator, you can enjoy his gifts. It might even make you feel closer to your higher power to admire and appreciate his creations. I call that a spiritual experience—where you feel the safety, peace, and utter calm of knowing you are not alone. Who can marvel at the ocean without feeling that?

WHAT A PIECE OF WORK IS MAN

I go walking, and the hills loom above me, range upon range, one against the other. I cannot tell where one begins and another leaves off. But when I talk with God, He lifts me up where I can see clearly, where everything has a distinct contour.

—MADAM CHIANG KAI-SHEK

If you think about how admiring (instead of trying to alter) God's creations (like your husband) makes you feel a divine presence, then you can begin to see how surrendering can make you feel closer to God. The more you admire your husband's magnificence and how everything about him is just as it should be, the more you will feel God's presence. The more you feel God's presence, the closer and more real your association and connection with Him. Faith and intimacy with your husband is a manifestation of your faith and intimacy with God.

Hiring a Higher Power

*W*hat if you don't believe in a power greater than you?

You will have to find one.

Look around for clues that there is someone more powerful than you. Go down to the ocean and try to order it around. Stand in the middle of a wheat field and try to make it still. The same force that's there is watching out for you, your husband, and your children.

When I first started my spiritual journey fourteen years ago, I had to act as if I believed there was a higher power when I wasn't really convinced that there was one. I had rejected the God of my childhood for being too neglectful, punishing, and insensitive. I couldn't find his compassion. In retrospect, I was probably transferring qualities that I disliked in my parents onto this God. Nevertheless, I fired the God I had been brought up with and I wrote about what I wanted in a higher power and decided that he existed for me; I had faith that he would show me the way. It worked.

Here's what I believe to be true: My higher power is a creative, humorous, compassionate Spirit that is manifested in my life through other people and my own inner voice. I get plenty of generous gifts from Spirit, including my wonderful husband, my beautiful home, the inspiration to write, and the friendship of incredible women. I choose my own path, and Spirit honors my decisions, even if they are not in my best interest. Sometimes I meet unpleasant consequences this way, but Spirit is always there to show me what to do next. Spirit knows about my sadness and comforts me when I cry.

I can hear Spirit best when I am quiet and introspective. I have a hard time connecting with Spirit when I'm afraid of the future. When I take time for solitude and meditation, care for myself, stay in gratitude and trust that Spirit is taking care of me, things seem to flow more easily. I find more laughter and joy in my day when I tune into Spirit. Spirit often tells me that he made this day for me, and that he wants me to enjoy it. I know that I'm precious to Spirit, and this makes me feel safe. I thank Spirit regularly and I try to remember that Spirit has made this day, and so in my eyes it is wonderful.

24

LET HIM SOLVE SOME
OF YOUR PROBLEMS

> *"We seldom attribute common sense except to those who
> agree with us."*
> — La Rochefoucauld

*What are you having trouble with in your life? Ask
your husband what he thinks you should do, and be
prepared to follow through with his suggestion. Instead of
negotiating by arguing with him, tell him what you want
and don't want, how you feel and what your limits are.*

*Why carry all of life's burdens yourself when your
husband is there, ready and willing to solve problems on
your behalf? Admitting that you don't know what to do in
every situation will actually make you stronger, not weaker,
as you absorb his strength and wisdom for your benefit.*

The Training Method was one of my more subversive (yet ineffective) tactics for controlling my husband. I (wrongly) assumed that I could *train* John to give the right answer (my answer) to any question just by setting him up so that essentially, all he would have to do is fill in the blank. The friction that this caused, of course, was off the charts. That's because if he gave the "wrong" answer (something other than what I thought), I simply told him the "right" answer (what I thought), hoping he would eventually start to think like me.

He didn't. He grew irritated.

Here's an example:

> ME: Do you think we should get a new water heater? (Me asking the "setup" question)
>
> HIM: No, the old one's working fine, and we can wait to replace it until something goes wrong. (Him, saying what he thinks and unwittingly giving the "wrong" answer)
>
> ME: I was thinking that we should just replace it now since we know it's on its last leg. That way, we can avoid a crisis. (Me arguing with what he thinks)
>
> HIM: It doesn't seem like a priority right now. Those things can last a long time. (Him defending his position)
>
> ME: I think you're asking for trouble by just waiting around for the whole thing to fall apart. It'll leak all over the carpet and leave us with no hot water for days. Why would you want to do that? (Me insulting him)
>
> HIM: I don't think that's going to happen. (Him defending himself)

ME: Well you should think these things through. (Me further criticizing him)

Gee, I wonder why that bugged him?

The reason I asked John what to do was not because I wanted *his* opinion, but because I didn't want to be alone in my opinion. I wrongly thought that intimacy resulted from our both thinking the same thing. I was also hoping that he might offer to take initiative (i.e., call the water heater company to schedule and oversee the installation), so I wouldn't have to do everything. I was longing for that partnership I'd heard marriage could be, and I thought that discussing decisions—big or small—would contribute to intimacy. Instead, these conversations just proved how little I respected him.

John's a man, so that means he doesn't think like me. Thank goodness for that, because I'd probably get bored and lonely living with myself. On the downside, it took me quite a while to stop trying to "train" him and actually regard his answers as wise. At first, every time he said something that I disagreed with, it fortified my belief that he wasn't really somebody I could depend on. I probably should have just married myself and saved us both a lot of trouble.

A SOURCE OF ELEGANT SOLUTIONS

I don't ask my husband to solve all of my problems, of course. Many of the challenges I come up against I can and do handle myself. At times when I'm stuck, however, I've found that John's a tremendous resource. I had simply never learned to take advantage of his help until I surrendered.

Those of us who have been controlling for so long have a hard time making this transition. We were so used to taking care of everything by ourselves that it just didn't occur to us to reach out to our husbands for help. Add to that our unwillingness to do things any way but our way, and you have a steely, independent existence, even when we are married to smart, capable men. In reality, we don't ask for help because we don't want to be vulnerable: to risk that our husbands would make costly mistakes, or worse, to find out that they wouldn't or couldn't help us.

Not until I surrendered could I see that I was throwing away something I had once valued: his ideas. I decided to try to listen to them, even if I didn't like them. Sometimes the ideas would scare me, but by clearly expressing my desires and feelings, and by acting in faith, I could compromise and avoid crushing intimacy. The same has been true for other women.

For instance, my friend Phoebe was frustrated that the backyard of her new house was covered with hundreds of paving stones where she wanted a lawn. It was expensive to have them removed, and they were too numerous to move herself. So, Phoebe told her husband she wanted a lawn in the backyard and asked him what he thought they should do with all the paving stones.

Phoebe secretly wanted to hire someone to bring a dump truck to the house and was hoping her husband would suggest it. Instead, he proposed that they advertise in a local paper that they were offering free paving stones to anyone who would come and get them. Inside, Phoebe cringed at the idea of trying to give away paving stones that were in her backyard because she didn't think anyone would want them. Nevertheless, she went along with his idea.

People showed up in droves, happy to pry up their own stones to take with them. The following week, Phoebe had a dirt yard, ready for a new lawn. She hadn't had to do or pay a thing, and she appreciated that her husband's solution was a happier, more ecologically sound one than filling the local landfill. Suddenly, she remembered why she admired her husband in the first place.

Remember, if you're going to ask your husband for input, be prepared to hear his response and go along with it. Don't let your preconceived notions prejudice you against his ideas. After all, if you ask his opinion, then do something else, why did you bother? It would have been more honest to tell him what you wanted to do, rather than asking an open-ended question. Be open to his answers, rather than rejecting them immediately. Really hear him.

NEW AND IMPROVED NEGOTIATIONS

> *"Never go to bed angry. Stay up and fight."*
> — PHYLLIS DILLER

Maybe you've rejected your husband's answers in the past because you were afraid he was wrong. Maybe you just wanted to stay in control. Perhaps you were testing him (like I used to) to see if he knew the "right" answer. Perhaps you thought you were smarter than him.

Recognize that honoring his answers takes the same amount of courage that trusting him does.

Honoring his thoughts and ideas doesn't mean that you can't have a conversation—just don't argue with his thinking. Instead, stick to telling him how you feel and what you want. Be direct. (See Chapter 5: Express Your Desires) Remember that how you feel influences your husband's thinking, just as his thinking will also color how you feel. If he thinks you should wait to get new carpet until after all the painting is done and you don't want to, you can say so. If he still thinks you should, then wait.

You won't die from having old carpet for another month or two, but you could kill the intimacy in your marriage by disregarding what he thinks so you can have your way. Is it worth that? He may change his mind once he hears what you want, so don't be afraid to share your feelings. His first reaction is not necessarily his best thinking, so let the conversation run its course.

But in the end, accept his position. Remember that your goal is to bring intimacy to your marriage and to get out of the lonely trap. Your goal is *not* to be right all the time. It is *not* to get exactly what you want when you want it. When you argue, you're heading toward the wrong goal.

Deferring to my husband was the hardest part of surrendering for me. I know that I'm smart and I didn't see why I should have to go along with what he thought just to avoid an argument. Why shouldn't *he* defer to my thinking to preserve intimacy? I spent some time hating the whole idea of doing what he thought was right when I disagreed. Then, as I started to rely on his thinking more, I began to see this new arrangement as a form of negotiation that felt better than steamrollering him. For example, the day before I planned to be a guest on a talk-radio show in Los Angeles, John and I had a negotiation that went like this:

HIM: Maybe you should leave at 8:00 instead of 8:30 to get to the radio show on time. (Him saying what he thinks)

ME: I don't want to leave that early. (Me stating what I want or don't want)

HIM: Still, you never know about traffic between here and L.A., and it would be a shame to miss any of the show because you were late. I think it's better to be safe than sorry. (Him saying what he thinks)

ME: That's true, but I feel safe allowing an hour-and-a-half. (Me saying how I feel)

HIM: You may be right, but I think it's better to be early than risk being late. (Him saying what he thinks)

ME: Okay. It can't hurt. I'll leave at 8:00.

Granted, I acquiesced this time, but the conversation was a true negotiation. In other words, I didn't just dismiss, contradict, or criticize him. We both stated our positions, and I didn't need to argue, because I knew he was taking into account what I wanted and how I felt. The old conversation (which is less about negotiation and more about control) would have gone like this:

HIM: Maybe you should leave at 8:00 instead of 8:30 to get to the radio show on time. (Him saying what he thinks)

ME: Don't be ridiculous. It won't take that long to get to L.A. (Me dismissing him)

HIM: It's not ridiculous. Sometimes traffic is terrible. (Him defending himself)

ME: Still, it can't take two hours to get there! (Me contradicting him)

HIM: How do you know? (Him taking the offensive with me)

ME: I have it under control so just let me handle it okay? (Me discouraging his help in the future)

Now, instead of making every decision by myself, I have created a safe space for John to share his opinions with me without worrying that I will attack him. In return, I have the reassurance of knowing that someone else is thinking of ways to lighten my load or make things more pleasant for me. When John helps me, I can feel his love and concern. Because I am not trying to control the situation, I have no doubt that he is putting my interest first. That brings about the most intense connection between us, one that is so gratifying that I can actually feel my love for him grow. Instead of keeping him and his "nutty" ideas at arm's length, I embrace him and employ his ideas. I'm reminded that we're a team, and that we're in this world together.

What could be more intimate than that?

25

BE A DIPLOMAT
IN THE MALE CULTURE

> *"Saying that men talk about baseball in order to avoid talking about their feelings is the same as saying that women talk about their feelings in order to avoid talking about baseball."*
> —DEBORAH TANNEN

Forget the notion that "more communication" is the key to an intimate marriage. Some things that are perfectly reasonable to discuss with women are not so comfortable for men. Talking about feelings is not a popular pastime in the male culture, so to be polite, don't ask about them, but continue to share yours. Generally, men talk far less each day than women, so don't expect your husband to want to talk as much as you.

The truth is, the less you communicate your complaints, negative thoughts, and criticisms to your husband, the better your intimacy will be, and the stronger your marriage. Withholding information from your husband may feel dishonest, but it's really being mature and polite.

Men have a culture all their own and being a diplomat in it will improve domestic relations dramatically.

*Y*ou may have been told, as I was, that the key to a good marriage is communication. I thought that this meant getting my husband to share his feelings about every issue that affected him and telling him my every thought. That included when I thought he was wrong, when I didn't approve of his outfit, his coarseness, or his lack of concern about our future.

I was just communicating my honest feelings, and if some communication is good, more communication is better, right?

Wrong.

Think of all the couples you know who communicated constantly—right up to the day they went to court to communicate through their lawyers. Think of all the conversations you've had with your partner where you were "communicating" as best you could and at the end you were ready to kill each other. Although I have a degree in communications, trying for years to "communicate" with my husband never got me the connection I craved.

HONOR LOCAL CUSTOMS

> *Reporter: What do you think of Western civilization?*
> *Gandhi: I think it's a great idea.*

*F*or some reason, it's much harder to extend diplomacy to our husbands than it is to honor customs in a foreign place. But I suggest that you revere the male culture if you want harmony in your marriage.

In communicating with your husband, the first thing you have to remember is that men have a different culture from women. Unlike women who are constantly talking about their feelings, sharing their secrets and embarrassments, frustrations and failures with each other, men have more terse relationships with their buddies. They don't often talk about their feelings, but rather their actions. So, when we overcommunicate with our husbands, and beg them to tell us what they are *feeling*, they have the sense that they have just landed on foreign ground—and generally it feels like enemy territory because they are being interrogated and bombarded.

Much like visiting another country, where I would honor the unfamiliar, relations seem to go more smoothly between my husband and me when I honor the male culture. Using diplomacy means remembering not to make fun of his culture or pressure him to do or say something that will make him uncomfortable.

NEVER ASK A MAN THIS QUESTION

"O Lord, please fill my mouth with worthwhile stuff, and nudge me when I've said enough."
—ANONYMOUS

Many women believe that they can have intimacy with a man just the way they'd have intimacy with another woman—by asking him to share his feelings. This tactic usually bombs because asking a man how he feels is like asking a woman about her weight. At best, it's uncomfortable, and at worst, it's embarrassing.

Never ask a man how he feels.

Prior to surrendering, I used to try to get John to express his feelings. He'd start out saying, "I think . . ." and I would correct him by saying, "You mean I feel!" He would roll his eyes and start again, desperate to give the right answer and end the torture. Next he'd say, "I feel like I . . ." I would jump in again and say, "When you feel 'like,' it's not a feeling."

Needless to say, his response was not the tender revelation I'd been hoping for.

The intimacy came when I least expected it, like the time he wanted to show me the lunar eclipse and put his arms around me to keep me warm while he explained how much of the moon would eventually be in shadow. He didn't tell me how he felt, but the closeness was palpable. I didn't have to get that moment started by drawing out his feelings.

Intimacy does *not* require that your husband tell you how he feels. Look for and enjoy it elsewhere, and censor your criticisms to keep relations smooth and friendly. You may never feel "at home" in the male culture since it's not your native environment, but you can learn to get along in it.

EXPRESS YOUR SELF IN TERMS OF FEELINGS

Just because he's not necessarily expressing his feelings doesn't mean that you shouldn't express yours. Tuning into and expressing your feelings will help you negotiate clearly, connect emotionally and stay feminine. This is a gift to your husband, because in the male culture, feelings are not as prominent. For instance, instead of saying, "The dog two doors down seems vicious. I think he might attack the children." You would say, "I'm scared of that dog that lives two-doors down." He'll be able to hear you better when he knows how you feel than he would if he had to debate with you about what you think.

A surrendered wife might tell her husband any of the following:

1. "I'm afraid of the neighbor." (rather than "I think the neighbor is not a nice man.")
2. "I feel guilty about eating all that chocolate." (rather than, "I know it isn't good for me to eat too much chocolate. I shouldn't have done it.")
3. "I'm excited about moving into a new house." (rather than, "Moving to the new house is going to be a big change for us, and that will be nice.")

Although men don't like to talk about *their* feelings, they have an easier time connecting to us when we use feeling sentences like the ones above. We're less likely to trigger a response from him to fix the situation or argue about it. For instance, in example number one he might naturally react to the nonfeeling statements by trying to downplay your judgments of the neighbor. You could actually end up fighting about whether the neighbor is a jerk or not, and really, who cares? You'd no doubt be happier if he just heard that you were angry or scared and sympathized with you. With example number two, he might try to help you come up with a method for not eating too much chocolate—which could be hurtful and irritating for you—if he heard only the latter statement. With example number three, he would be glad to hear of your excitement, but might take the other statement as a complaint that he doesn't make you happy. See how important it is to stay close to your feelings and express them?

THE TRUTH ABOUT TELLING THE TRUTH

"Politeness is the art of selecting among one's real thoughts."
—MADAME DE STAËL

The truth is, there are some things you are better off *not* communicating with your spouse. The less you communicate hurtful truths and criticisms, the better your intimacy will be, and the stronger your marriage. This is the same treatment you'd give a friend who had put on weight or gotten an awful haircut—you would use manners and discretion.

I often hear women justifying their lack of diplomacy by saying, "But it's the truth! He *did* choose terrible stocks to invest in! He *did* pick his teeth at the governor's ball!"

The truth is, it's not always such a great idea to tell your husband the truth. Sure it feels good to be right. Everyone likes to feel smart, and saying "I told you so" is undeniably satisfying. But in my experience, this kind of satisfaction is not worth the price of admission because it puts distance between my partner and me. If you would rather snuggle and giggle in bed together than stay up late arguing, don't tell him those kinds of truths. Your husband deserves the same diplomacy and grace that you would offer to any stranger next to you in a waiting room.

Today you won't catch *me* asking John how he feels about anything. He doesn't like it, and I never got what I was hoping for when I asked. Now, I'd rather focus on and express how I feel, since I'm the female in this relationship. I once asked John if he would object if nobody ever asked him how he felt again.

I bet you can guess what he said.

26

MEASURE YOUR
PROGRESS

> *"Success in life consists of going from one mistake to the next without losing enthusiasm."*
> —WINSTON CHURCHILL

When you feel discouraged about surrendering and think you're not making any progress, look for signs that things are changing. Has your husband done anything out of the ordinary lately? Do you have more energy than you used to? Do you take better care of yourself? Do you have fewer responsibilities? Does your husband look different? Do you feel more intimate? Write down everything that reflects your progress, rather than your mistakes. This will fuel you as you journey on.

You should start to see improvement after two weeks, so if you don't, go back and review the basics. How's your self-care? Have you said "ouch" when he hurts your feelings? Are you expressing your desires? Have you relinquished inappropriate control?

*W*hen your husband starts to feel respected, he will feel a new strength. This will lead him to do things that he might not have done in the past because he feared your criticism. You may feel like you're losing control over him, which you are. This is a good thing—even if it doesn't seem that way.

The first month of surrendering was murder for Kim. She felt things were worse, not better.

One day her husband, Rick, confessed that he'd gone to see a doctor about getting surgery to correct his vision. She was shocked that he hadn't told her first, especially since she had indicated that she felt the surgery was too expensive. Rick admitted that he had kept his plans from her because he didn't want to invoke her wrath or be controlled. Kim felt deceived, and complained to me that this didn't seem like progress towards intimacy.

When I asked Kim how she would have felt if her husband had gone to look at a new lawn mower without telling her, she admitted that she wouldn't have cared. The *true* reason she was upset about Rick's "deceit" was not because he hadn't told her beforehand, but because her husband was not letting her control him like he had in the past. She wasn't upset because she felt he was hiding things from her, but because she disapproved of the expense and risk of surgery. Kim was still trying to enforce her values on Rick, and it wasn't working. She veiled her control to try to reestablish her rule.

In the old days, perhaps Rick would not have done something he knew she disapproved of because he would have wanted to keep the peace. In the new environment, he was willing to risk her disapproval because he had gained some strength from being respected. This is a good thing, but it didn't seem that way to Kim.

Although surrendering does result in immediate benefits—like more time to yourself, less responsibility and greater intimacy—losing control can feel like a big drawback. I could tell by Rick's bold initiative that Kim had been respecting him more, but I had a hard time convincing her that this was progress. Kim's new respect, however flawed, helped Rick tap into his own power and do what seemed right to him. He probably would not have done so had Kim not surrendered first. His trip to the eye doctor was a way of reminding them both that he was in charge of himself.

Buckle Up for the Roller Coaster Ride

"You are always on your way to a miracle."
—Sark

*W*hat if things seem worse and not better, then what? How can you tell if your surrendering is actually working? Here's a general overview of what the whole process looks like so you know what to expect. Your experience will probably be something like this, although it may not be in the same order:

1. You hear or read about surrendering. You think, "That sounds awful!" but a lingering curiosity leads you to find out more. You examine yourself to see if you're controlling, and feel a mixture of relief and dread when you realize that you *are*—but perhaps you aren't as bad as some other women.

2. You start to be respectful, mind your own business, and focus on your own self-care for a few days. This feels good. You have a sense of accomplishment, and life seems more balanced.

3. Your husband suddenly reacts with some mistrust, surprise, or trepidation. He doesn't say anything directly, but you can tell he's wondering about the changes. This is almost insulting, since all you're doing is being nice, and you weren't *that* bad before . . . were you?

4. You're tempted to tell your husband that you really are changing, but instead you wisely say nothing and continue surrendering.

5. Your husband suddenly seems to be in touch with his inner jerk. You wonder what in the world is the matter with him, and feel especially indignant because you've been treating him so well. You realize that you are shaking things up, that he's off balance, and you feel a sort of perverse resolve to stay the course of surrendering.

6. He's gotten through that funk, and now you're noticing that he looks different. People are asking him if he's lost weight or gotten a haircut, but you know that he's emanating confidence and that has changed his appearance. You feel proud and happy about this. Perhaps the most dramatic change is that he's taken over the finances without any help from you. Should you be worried? You talk to your friends about it. They ask you if you've lost your mind. Then you talk to surrendered friends about it. They tell you to trust. Good advice.

7. You feel strangely tongue-tied and restless for a period. You're speaking very little because you're not controlling him anymore. You wonder if you actually have anything to say. What do

married people talk about anyway? After making so much noise for so long you realize you haven't even been able to hear your own heart. You need support from other women. You call and ask them how to figure out what it is you want.

8. Your husband is still resisting the new culture. He asks you what he should wear, or tries to get you to take the finances back or throws out other kinds of bait that absolutely drive you batty. You are on the edge and sliding off. You can't believe you married such a wimpy, whiny guy with no mind of his own. Then, after resisting it five times, you take the bait the sixth time. You want to eat worms.

9. It's two or three weeks since you started surrendering and you are definitely noticing the buds of new intimacy. You're playful like kids. He told you he wanted to ask you to marry him all over again. You hold hands, talk about the future, and feel intense closeness. Things are peaceful. In your heart, you know that you have done something remarkable. It seems like a miracle.

10. Hubby seems in a funk again. He's hiding in what John Gray would call "his cave" and brooding. You're tempted to rescue him, but you don't. You get the chance to affirm that he is a wonderful husband, provider, and father. Now he's introspective as he does some inner shifting to catch up with you. You wish he would snap out of it so you wouldn't be tempted to ask him what's wrong.

11. Your man is suddenly holding himself to higher standards. He's more focused on what you want, thinks he can make more money, wants to give the kids a better spiritual foundation. You're impressed and amazed. Who knew he was like this? You feel more gratitude.

12. You completely flub surrendering and tell him everything he should be doing differently. And you don't even care. Whatever he just did was the last straw. You question the wisdom of surrendering to a man like him. You wonder if maybe this only works for other people and not you. A friend reminds you that you haven't done much self-care. Oh yeah. Maybe that will help restore your sanity.

13. You went back to basics—gratitude, respect, self-care—and your marriage seems much better, much more hopeful. Perhaps you won't have to file for divorce—not today anyway. You remember to say "ouch" the next time he hurts your feelings, and he actually seems to care.

14. Yes, things are definitely improving. He got a promotion or bonus at work! He feels good about himself, you feel good about yourself and him. Together you're unstoppable. Obviously this is a match made in heaven. How could you ever have doubted it?

15. You go in and out of surrendering. Some days are bliss and some are disasters. Still, overall surrendering seems to have a positive impact. Even the kids seem calmer. You never quite lose that part of you that thinks he is just so different. For this, you can be glad.

Did that sound like a roller coaster? I hope you're not too dizzy, but it's important to realize that surrendering is not a linear course, but rather a series of ups and downs that ultimately slopes upward. The most important thing to keep in mind is that when you're at stage twelve and feeling terrible, you are still way ahead of where you were at stage two when you were feeling good.

LEAVING NORMAL

※

> *"You gain strength, courage and confidence by every experience in which you really stop to look fear in the face . . . You must do the thing you think you cannot do."*
> — ELEANOR ROOSEVELT

So how do you stay motivated? In time, you'll have the validation and the reinforcement of a healthy, intimate, romantic relationship to keep you motivated. Early on, however, the most obvious validation you'll get that you're surrendering (besides the pats on the back from other surrendered wives) is that your mate will do things he never did before. For instance, one woman told me her husband had called a travel agent, even though he had never before even planned a vacation. My husband started using a day-planner religiously. Neither of these actions constitutes the ninth wonder of the world, but both were departures from what these husbands *normally* did. This unusual and attractive behavior is at least partly the result of feeling a new freedom. Since their wives weren't criticizing them, these men were taking responsibility for themselves.

EXPECT GROWING PAINS

"The art of love is largely the art of persistence."
—ALBERT ELLIS

 Since I could see how *he* was acting differently, I supposed that everybody could see that I was acting differently too. Boy, was I disappointed!

Early in my surrendering, a close family friend came to stay with us. I asked him if he could see the difference in my behavior. "I can't see any difference in how you act," he told me, "but I can sure see the difference in John. He seems so much more alive."

I wasn't surrendering perfectly, but I knew my behavior had changed. Still, nobody was standing up to cheer me on. This was disappointing because I was making a Herculean effort to change. I wanted credit! I wanted John to say, "Honey, thank you for surrendering. I think you are doing a terrific job, and I love you more now than ever."

Instead, we were both feeling some growing pains.

Imagine that the two of you are learning to speak French. You spend ten hours the first week listening to tapes and reading a book, and by the end of the week you've got a few phrases down. Your husband hasn't put as much time in, so when you try to practice what you've learned with him, he stares at you blankly. He might even get frustrated and angry with you for trying to speak to him in a language he doesn't understand. Of course you could revert to English. Or, you might wisely choose to continue speaking to him in French and wait for him to catch on. The problem with taking the first option is that you end up right back where you were—in a marriage that is lonely and doesn't meet your needs. The problem with the second version is that it requires incredible patience and faith.

I'm not a patient person, so when my husband was in a funk not too long ago, I attacked him about it. I said, "What's the matter with you? If you're not reading the paper, you're watching television, listening to the radio, or taking a nap!" Then I tacked on an "I miss you" at the end because just then I remembered that I'm trying to be a surrendered wife, and the truth was, I did miss him: his company, his lively conversations, his happy moods. When I finished, he stared at me blankly, shrugged his shoulders, and said he was too tired to talk about it. I might as well have been mooing like a cow for all the good it did me.

Luckily, I discussed this issue with a friend who reminded me that I needed to tend to my own self-care and give him the space to solve his own problems. Sure enough, as soon as I did what she suggested, I noticed my husband seemed more available. Once he got the hang of the latest changes in our relationship, everything was fine.

NO MATTER HOW FAST YOU GROW, HE'LL CATCH UP WITH YOU

One of the big fears I had about making changes was that I would upset the balance in my marriage and end up alone. I found that the other surrendered wives shared a similar notion. We erroneously believed that if we grew too much, our husbands would not be able to keep up. We were motivated to stay stuck where we were, even if it wasn't very comfortable, because we were afraid we'd lose our marriages.

I'm pleased to report that our experience has been that no matter how quickly we take action and no matter how dramatic our growth, our husbands always seem to keep pace with us. Remember: Marriage is like water, we seek our own level.

So the path of surrendering is a little bumpy. First you grow. Then he resists. But eventually he grows to match you. You start to trust him to do more and he panics at first. Then he feels his own power and strength as he succeeds. And you feel it, too.

You may feel lonely when your husband is in a funk. You'll probably miss him and wax nostalgic for the good old days. Remind yourself that if the good old days had really been that good, you wouldn't have bought or borrowed this book and read it. Stay on course and the rewards will be great. If you fear that your marriage is dying, you're probably right. Be patient and a better, stronger union will bloom in its place.

27

SPEND YOUR ENERGY SURPLUS ON YOURSELF

"There is only one corner of the universe you can be certain of improving, and that's your own self."
—ALDOUS HUXLEY

If surrendering makes you feel like you have nothing to do or say anymore, that's a good measure of how much time you spent in Needless Emotional Turmoil. Now that you have a surplus of time and energy to spend on yourself, try to recall what it was that you always wished you had time to do, but never could, whether it was reading a magazine cover-to-cover, watching a mindless TV show, or painting with watercolors.

Uncovering your own passion will contribute to intimacy by making you more attractive and vibrant. Spending your surplus energy on yourself is about more than just maintaining balance: It's about making sure you become the woman you've always wanted to be.

*P*rior to surrendering, most of the wives I met had spent a lot of time and energy in Needless Emotional Turmoil, or NET for short. Once we stopped needlessly worrying about our husbands, we suddenly had an unfamiliar (and uncomfortable) energy surplus.

Shortly after she began surrendering, Susan was not sure what to do with all her free time now that she wasn't doing everything herself. Carolyn realized that since she wasn't going to talk about money, she had nothing to talk about when she went out to dinner with her husband. Ironically, these women experienced a sense of loss, and in a way, they *had* lost something: Where their space was once filled with familiar obsession and the usual worries, there was now a vacuum.

Without NET, life can be downright boring. There's no more telling your husband what to do or instructing him on things you think he should have done differently. There isn't much drama or fighting, and without that life can be dull, dull, dull.

Surviving Weightlessness

*I*magine you are carrying a backpack that's full of NET related to your husband. Imagine you are putting on this backpack every day and suddenly you stop. You will feel a little weightless at first. Maybe you would consider picking it up again out of habit, but you realize that you don't want to schlep it around all day, and you don't want anything that's in it. Then as you make the choice to leave it where it is rather than put it on, you might feel insecure and awkward, but also light and unburdened. Throughout the day little surges of panic might pulse through your body when you notice you're not wearing the backpack, as if you'd forgotten something important.

Remind yourself that you're not supposed to be wearing that backpack, and that it's okay to leave it off. Notice how much more you can do and how much faster you can move without it.

When you first experience an energy surplus from not wearing a backpack full of NET about what your husband is doing, you may also notice other feelings coming up. For example, you may feel you have nothing in common with your husband anymore because there's nothing to argue about. Also, as your focus moves from him to you, perhaps you'll have some dissatisfaction with some other aspects of your life. Maybe you'll notice you're frustrated with the way your kids worm out of their chores or you'll be upset with yourself that you haven't been more proactive in your career. Maybe you'll feel annoyed about how the garden is totally overgrown with weeds when it used to be your pride and joy.

When you start to become more aware of aspects of *your* life that you want to improve that aren't related to your husband, that means you're shifting your focus off of him and on to you. You've stopped distracting yourself with his problems and started to face your own. If this is the case, be sure to pat yourself on the back for doing such a good job surrendering.

The Joy of Accomplishing Absolutely Nothing

"To mature is in part to realize that while complete intimacy and omniscience and power cannot be had, self-transcendence, growth, and closeness to others are nevertheless within one's reach."
— Sissela Bok

As soon as you finish patting yourself on the back, start a new project. Make a quilt or a new friend. Read a novel or write one of your own. Join a gym or a theater group. Take a class or a trip. Walk in the woods or in a park. Do anything that makes you happy or interests you, even if it means getting a baby-sitter or spending money. You're now taking self-care a step further. Don't worry so much about what you accomplish, but rather measure your success by how happy and fulfilled your new project makes you feel. Before I surrendered, I always wished I could spend more time with my four-year-old nephew, Josh (who reminds me not to take life too seriously) and have long lunches with my girlfriends. Now I see Josh every week, dawdle with girlfriends at the sushi bar and take naps to boot. It's not overly productive, but it makes me happy.

SPARKLING DINNER CONVERSATION

What does doing something you enjoy have to do with being intimate with your husband? For one thing, getting involved in your own life distracts you from the temptation to take a bite of Really Big Bait. More importantly, your new activities will re-awaken your passion for life. Remember, though, that what feeds your spirit may not move your husband. Be sure to allow yourself your own passions, even if he does not share them. If you love skiing and he doesn't, join a ski club and set off every chance you get. If you enjoy foreign films and he hates subtitles, go with a friend. If you need to rumba and he won't dance, sign up for a class at the local college. When you're engaged in your interests, you're also more attractive and fun to be around. When you feel good, you're more likely to be grateful and respectful instead of nitpicky and critical. Plus, you will have new experiences and stories to share with your husband over dinner.

As a wonderful fringe benefit to making yourself happy, you will also be making someone else you love happy: your husband. He will never feel better about himself or more attracted to you than when he sees you smiling, fulfilled, and excited. He may even follow your example and pursue his own passions. Then he'll have something interesting to talk about at dinner too.

FIND THE COURAGE TO PURSUE YOUR AMBITIONS

"Until you value yourself, you won't value your time. Until you value your time, you will not do anything with it."
— M. SCOTT PECK

Once Tess quit worrying needlessly about her husband, she had to face that she had been avoiding her ambition to write children's books. When she first noticed her energy surplus she felt a sense of sadness. Outside of being a mom, her life seemed unimportant. She made a decision to devote an hour or two each day to writing new stories and putting finishing touches on old ones. Tess shared what she wrote with friends and family, and asked for feedback about how she could improve. Everyone agreed her work was wonderful, and encouraged her to pursue getting it published.

And then the terror set in. Being the armchair critic of her husband's life had felt far less scary than sending her stories out to publishers and agents. Focusing on her passion brought up Tess's fear of rejection, and understandably so. Without the distraction of worrying about her husband and controlling him, Tess was stuck with facing *her* challenges.

Once she found the courage to take risks in her own life, Tess was amazed at how supportive her husband became. His enthusiasm and pride for her writing reminded her of just how much he wanted her to be happy.

Your husband may surprise you with his enthusiastic support for your interests, too. One woman learned that her husband didn't mind staying at home with the kids so she could go out with her girlfriends. Another woman was impressed that her husband spent most of the weekend doing heavy digging so she could plant vegetables and flowers in her garden. I was moved to learn that John didn't mind helping me baby-sit my young nephew on Saturday nights because he knows the boy's silliness and innocence lift my spirits.

These are ordinary husbands I'm writing about who are probably not much different from yours. One of the things that gave them enormous pleasure was watching the women they love blossom with the discovery of new interests and talents.

So, put that Needless Emotional Turmoil in a backpack and send it off to the dump. Remember, if you find yourself longing for distraction and drama, you can always pick a fight with your husband. Somehow, when your life is full of other passion and pleasure, that temptation simply goes away.

How It Is Now

To love someone deeply gives you strength. Being loved by
someone deeply gives you courage.

— LAO-TZU

*I*t was an ordinary day, when I realized that surrendering had done its job.

John and I were out to breakfast at a small café and I felt incredibly relaxed. He opened doors for me—the front door of our home, the car door, the entrance to the cafe. In the crowded waiting area, my shy husband approached a couple and asked permission to take an empty chair. He pulled it up and held it out so that I could sit down. Then he asked me if I wanted some juice. I smiled and said, "yes, please" and he brought me a glass of golden, freshly squeezed juice.

We didn't win a million dollars and the heavens didn't open up. But that day, John and I were both conscious of a shift. Our lives had changed. I had finally made friends with receiving graciously, and John was responding with a willingness to take care of me. We were yin and yang and I felt the power of our differences and togetherness. I knew that we could never go back to the old way.

A Symbol of New Marriage

Ironically, since I started respecting my husband, he seems so much more worthy of my esteem. On our ninth anniversary, I decided to adopt John's last name. In our old marriage, I had kept my maiden name as a symbol of my identity as a feminist. Perhaps on some level, I was also reluctant and terrified to merge with my husband. In our *new marriage*, however, I wanted to do something that symbolized my profound respect for him and acknowledged our intimacy and oneness.

While I don't do this surrendering thing perfectly, I now enjoy being married to my wonderful, handsome, capable husband. Today, I have the intimate marriage I always dreamed was possible.

If you surrender to your husband, you will too.

Really.

APPENDIX

SURRENDERED CIRCLES

The very first Surrendered Circle met on a Thursday afternoon in November 1998. Four of my friends—a massage therapist, a teacher, and two full-time mothers—and I had been practicing the principles of the surrendered wife when we started our group. I invited these women to my house for a pot-luck and to form a community of women who would support each other in surrendering. I felt fortunate because surrendering is hard to do alone: Mutual support is a key ingredient. Thus, Surrendered Circles were born.

This chapter is intended as a handbook for starting your own Surrendered Circle. Meeting once a month—either in person or online—with even just one other woman will help keep you on the path to a more fulfilling, intimate marriage.

SAFETY COMES FIRST

In the first Surrendered Circle, we laughed and cried, ate and talked, and somehow found safety and healing with each other's help. From the very first meeting, we felt a tremendous bond. No matter how discouraged and hopeless we were when we arrived, we always left energized and optimistic. We called each other frequently during the month for encouragement and strength.

Of course, if you are going to expose your problems and fears, missteps and hopes, creating a safe space in the circle has to be the top priority. In other words, the individuals in the group must promise to keep the stories they hear within the circle confidential.

The gathering is sacred. Do not treat it as anything less. Criticism and gossip have no place among the members of the Surrendered Circle. Only positive feedback is appropriate.

You are qualified to host a Surrendered Circle regardless of how long you've been practicing or how little you think you know. You won't know all the answers when you have your first circle, but that doesn't matter because the magic of these groups is not dependent on the host, but on the collective wisdom of women who want to transform themselves and their marriages. Together, you will find solutions.

Our Surrendered Circle met only once a month, but yours could certainly convene more frequently. Any gathering place is fine, as long as it is private. Someone new should host the circle each time, regardless of whose home you meet in.

There's no rigid format to follow, but I've included the schedule my group followed and three examples of exercises we did just in case you need a jump start to get your group engaged. You may also come up with your own exercises, and if you do, don't forget to post them on the Web site so the rest of us can give them a try.

Our monthly meetings started at 12:30 P.M. with chatting and settling in and wrapped up by 2:30 P.M. We sat on my couches, dining room chairs and on the floor. I always arranged for us to have privacy and sometimes I lit a few candles to set a sacred mood. John went out with his buddies for hot dogs and beer.

One Format for a Surrendered Circle
12:45 P.M.

Choose a host to lead the group through the readings that are a part of this particular format.

The host can read the italicized sections out loud:

Hello and welcome to the Surrendered Circle. Would you join me in praying for wisdom and divine guidance at this meeting?

We are grateful for the opportunity to meet and talk in confidence. We ask that you would bless this meeting with your wisdom, your power, and your love. We pray for the courage and strength we will need to continue on the journey of becoming our best selves as we restore passion, intimacy, and peace in our marriages.

INTRODUCTION

Welcome to the Surrendered Circle, a community of women who gather to support each other in practicing the principles of a surrendered wife. Please make yourself comfortable.

First Meeting Only:
We will begin with brief introductions around the room. If you wish, you may quickly share with us your name, how long you've been married, the ages of your children, and how long you've been practicing the principles of a surrendered wife. I'll start . . .

Ongoing Meetings:
We will quickly introduce ourselves by going around the circle and saying our first names. I'll start . . .

PASS THE ASK-IT BASKET

This is the Q&A basket. If you have a question you would like addressed in the meeting, please write it down and we'll read it out loud later on. You may sign your name or remain anonymous.

MEDITATIVE READINGS ON SURRENDERING

Choose a group member to read each of the following three sections out loud:

READING 1: HOW WE KNEW WE NEEDED TO SURRENDER (MY FRIEND, CHRISTINE GORDON, WROTE THIS ONE).

We, who have chosen the path of the surrendered wife, gather in love, support, and friendship. Our path is a sacred one, and so we close our circle to gossip and criticism, keeping our hearts and minds open to one another. We open ourselves to health—physical, emotional, and spiritual.

The circle is an ancient symbol of marriage. The wedding ring itself reminds us of a commitment to a life never-ending. The circle marks a sacred boundary around a man and a woman who together form a new family. We are conscious of a society that has lost its footing on the marriage path. With God as our guide, we have discovered that surrendering in our marriages gives us a new freedom we had not known before.

For a wife to surrender means she is willing to release her grip on her husband's life, thereby making his own journey possible. We have found that marriage works best when we let our husbands be the men and fathers only they know how to be. Surrendering is a process of celebrating our femaleness—our God-given right to receive life's blessings of love, companionship, prosperity, and family life. We can fulfill our womanhood only when we give our husbands the freedom to stand tall in their manhood. In extricating our grip, we find we have renewed energy for life's many joys.

Here are some of the signs that told us it was time to surrender:

- Feeling superior to our husbands.
- "Henpecking" or disrespecting our husbands behind their backs—particularly in the company of other wives.
- Encouraging other wives to disrespect their husbands.
- Disrespecting our husbands publicly and privately.
- Often hearing ourselves say the words, "I told my husband . . ."
- Believing everything would be okay if our husbands would just do as we said.

- Compulsively looking for the worst in our husbands.
- Eavesdropping on our husbands' conversations to ensure everything was handled correctly.
- Feeling that there was only one adult in the family—us!
- Feeling overburdened in parenting our children.
- Increasing fear around family decisions.
- Doing for our husbands what they were capable of doing for themselves.
- Recurring anxiety and depression.
- Physical exhaustion, often including chronic illness.
- A loss of interest in sex by either partner.
- Increasing resentment and jealousy at their victories in life.
- Rejecting their gifts until they could no longer risk giving.
- Often fantasizing about divorce or life with a man who would better match us.
- Discounting the reasons we had chosen our husband in the first place.
- Feeling that our needs had gone unmet for so long that we lost hope.
- Inability to trust our husbands in even the smallest matter.
- Finding our obsession to control had become so loud that we could no longer hear the voice of God.

READING 2: WHAT WE DID TO SURRENDER TO OUR HUSBANDS

Taking the following actions resulted in miraculous changes in our marriages. Please note that we do not recommend them to women who are in physically abusive relationships, or whose husbands have an active addiction, such as alcoholism.

We have also found that telling our husbands about these practices, while very tempting, is counterproductive. Announcing to our husbands that we would now be trying to respect them was no improvement at all. We talked to other wives freely, but we found it was not in our best interest to talk about the practices of a surrendered wife with our husbands. Instead, we urge you to simply take these actions as best you can.

Here are the things that we did, to the best of our ability, to surrender to our husbands:

- We refrained from offering our husbands advice or teaching them how to do things.
- We released our inappropriate expectations for our husbands and focused on appreciating their gifts.
- We discussed our problems with other married women to gain perspective, and so that we didn't have to rely on our husbands as our only emotional support.
- We apologized for being disrespectful whenever we contradicted, criticized, or dismissed our husbands' thoughts and ideas.
- We refrained from asking our husbands to do things we wanted them to do.
- We concentrated on taking care of ourselves first, knowing that our own contentment was the key to a happy household.
- We listened to our husbands' problems without offering solutions, trusting that they would find their own.
- We refrained from doing things for our husbands that they were capable of doing themselves, such as buying their clothes or making appointments for them to see the doctor or dentist.
- We respected our husbands' approach to parenting, and their unique relationship with their children and stepchildren.
- We deferred to our husbands' thinking when we had conflicting opinions.
- We relinquished control of the household finances and relied on our husbands to give us what we need.
- We made ourselves sexually available to our husbands.

- We acknowledged our hurt feelings by saying "ouch," our loneliness by saying "I miss you," and our gratitude by saying "thank you."
- We practiced graciously and gratefully receiving from our husbands whenever possible.
- We followed their direction and leadership, except when to do so would cause us emotional or physical distress.
- We told our husbands what we wanted in the way of clothing, household items, babies, vacations, etc., and allowed them to provide those things for us.
- We prayed for wisdom and listened carefully so we could hear the answers.

READING 3: WHAT HAPPENED WHEN WE SURRENDERED

Once we relinquished control of our husbands, they seemed to take more pride in themselves as men, husbands, and fathers. We found we had changed too. Here are some of the changes we experienced as we practiced surrendering as best we could:

- We felt genuine admiration and respect for our husbands.
- We felt a sense of dignity that had eluded us when we were nagging, complaining, and criticizing our husbands.
- We developed deeper, more satisfying relationships with women.
- Harmony was restored in our families as conflict and fighting dropped dramatically.
- We found ourselves doing less and accomplishing more.
- Our children showed more respect for our mates and relied on them for guidance in a deeper way.
- We felt excitement and fear at the dramatic changes in our lives.
- We had more time for relaxation and pleasurable activities for ourselves.

- We felt the pleasure of connecting with our own femininity.
- We had less to worry about, more to be grateful for, and the passionate, romantic relationships we had always wanted.
- Sex became more frequent and more enjoyable.
- Our husbands started earning more money. Some received raises or performance bonuses while others found better-paying work.
- We received more gifts than ever before.
- We became more conscious and comforted that a higher power was guiding and protecting us. This connection made us feel joyful.

CHOOSE EITHER FORMAT A OR B

Format A: Host tells her personal story until 1:30

At this time one of the women in the circle tells her "story." This might include describing what she learned from watching her parents' marriage, her relationship with her father, her patterns in dating and relationships, things that had happened to her that could have caused her to feel terror, and the ways that she tried to control her husband. It's helpful and healing for the host to talk about how she began to surrender, what her process was like and most importantly, the changes she experienced in her marriage. The story should end with the host's hopes for the future and gratitude for the present.

(Note: The most important thing to remember when you are telling your story is to be honest. Take risks, and show more of yourself than you are comfortable revealing. Tell about things that are embarrassing or possibly even shameful to you. Use this as an opportunity to let the group know you. You will be amazed at the trust you build.)

This is also good practice for being intimate with your husband. As you share your story with someone else, you are practicing vulnerability, which is precisely what you'll need in your marriage.

Conclude by inviting the members to ask the host if she would like feedback. Remind the group that feedback should be strictly positive, such as what you could relate to, what touched you, or why you are grateful to hear it.

OR

> *Format B: Members study the book* The Surrendered Wife
> *until 1:30*

Each group member reads a page of the book aloud and comments briefly (2 or 3 minutes maximum) about what they just read. The group can decide to read a particular section, or make their way through the book sequentially.

EXERCISE OR Q&A FROM THE ASK-IT BASKET UNTIL 1:55

Choose an exercise (provided on the following pages), or read and discuss the questions in the Ask-It Basket.

CONCLUSION (END BY 2:00)

That's all the time we have, but I'd like to make a few announcements before we close. The next Surrendered Circle will be held here on _____ at 12:30. You can exchange numbers to call other surrendered wives before the next circle if you wish. Are there any other announcements? (If you're using the story format, ask who wants to host the next circle).

Let's close with a moment of silence in honor of the sanctity of marriage, and to pray that others would find peace in their homes.

EXERCISES

I. Receiving

This exercise is about learning to receive graciously, and taking ownership of our unique gifts. Perhaps we have been taught to be modest or not to get too full of ourselves when we get a compliment, but today we will work on accepting kind comments and acknowledging our own virtues in front of others.

First, take a minute to think of and write down a sincere compliment for the woman on your left.

We are going to go around the circle and each of you will have a chance to look the woman to your left in the eyes and give her a compliment. Practice meeting her gaze and doing your best to receive the compliment. I suggest you respond by saying, "thank you, that's true." Or, if you can't do that, at least say "thank you." DO NOT say anything to discount the compliment. If you need duct tape to put around your mouth, we have some available. Do your very best to receive the compliment graciously. Who would like to start?

Now I want you to take just a minute to think about your best physical feature and write that down. We are going to go around the circle and tell the women on our right what our best feature is. Do not whisper this, or put in modifiers such as "kind of" or "pretty good." Rather, I would prefer that you use words like gorgeous, outstanding, fabulous, and amazing, as in "I have a gorgeous face." Who would like to start?

II. Gratitude

You have exactly five minutes to write a gratitude list about your man. Think of as many things as you can that you are grateful for about him. When you are through, you can read it to the group if you choose. (Set a kitchen timer for five minutes.) Ready? Go!

Who would like to read theirs out loud? (Go around the circle and read lists.)

This exercise can be turned into a gift for your husband. Get a small journal or notebook with blank pages and write one thing from the list on each of the pages. Use colored pens or crayons to decorate the pages.

III. Relinquishing Control

The purpose of this exercise is to hone your listening skills and to practice giving up control and taking on the feminine role in the family.

Think of something in your life that's bothering you. It can be anything and need not be limited to a relationship issue. Find a partner in the room (preferably someone you don't already know) and spend five minutes talking about this problem, concern, or worry with your partner while she listens. Be as vulnerable as you can by letting her see your imperfections and shortcomings. When you're through, switch with your partner and listen to her problem.

As the listener your job is to avoid interrupting, offering advice, or sharing a similar experience of your own. This will relieve you of having to formulate a response and let you concentrate on hearing every word. Look the speaker in the eye, to let her know that you take what she's saying seriously and that you respect her.

Bonus: For a feminine approach, practice using the following phrases when you're discussing your problem:

1. I can't
2. I feel
3. I want

THE ELECTRONIC COMMUNITY OF
SURRENDERED WIVES

*If you are in an isolated area and find it difficult to meet with other women even once a month, then a good alternative for support is an electronic Surrendered Circle: a group that meets regularly on the Internet.

I host a Web site:

http://www.surrenderedwife.com.

You can learn about Surrendered Circles, post messages, questions, and success stories on an electronic bulletin board. If you start your own circle, be sure to post the contact information on the Web site so that other women nearby can find you. If nothing else, you can gather e-mail addresses and ask for advice on the site. This will help sustain you by connecting you to women throughout the world who are on this same path. I welcome your comments, questions, wisdom, and support.

For ongoing encouragement and the latest information about intimate relationship workshops, books, and support groups, subscribe to the Surrendered Success Stories newsletter at:

http://www.egroups.com/subscribe/surrenderedwife.

Remember, however difficult your journey, you are not alone.

ABOUT THE AUTHOR

Laura Doyle, a feminist and former shrew, leads Surrendered Wife workshops and speaks to women about reclaiming passion and intimacy in their relationships. Once a copywriter for a marketing firm, Doyle earned her journalism degree from San Jose State University. She lives in Costa Mesa, California, with John Doyle, her husband of eleven years.

www.simonsays.com/surrenderedwife
www.surrenderedwife.com